e South, their degradation and ostracism at the North—flew willingly and gallantly to the support of the national Government. Their sufferings, assistance privations, and trials
which makes up the history of a nation preserved — HON. R.B. ELLIOTT'S speach page 7.

WHAT YOU DENY TO ONE CLASS YOU SHALL DENY TO ALL
ONE CLASS
TO ALL
HON. R.B. ELLIOTT'S speach page 4.

EQUALITY

NAVY

BALLOT

CHARLES SUMNER.

ELLIOTT,
olina,
OF REPRESENTATIVES, JANUARY 6. 1874.

EQUALITY OF RIGHTS
IS THE FIRST OF RIGHTS.
Charles Sumner.

E TOIL FOR OUR OWN CHILDERN AND NOT FOR THOSE OF OTHERS.

So far as tested, it is difficult to say they are not as good soldiers, as any.
A. Lincoln Dec. 1863.

PUB. E. SACHSE & CO. 5 N. LIBERTY ST. BALTIMORE.

HE GENIUS OF FREEDOM.

le volume of human nature, by the hand of the Divinity itself, and can never be erased or obscured by mortal power.
Hon. Robert B. Elliott.

THE FREEDMEN'S BUREAU.—Drawn by A. R. Waud.—[See Page 467.]

MAKE GOOD THE PROMISES

RECLAIMING RECONSTRUCTION AND ITS LEGACIES

Edited by

Kinshasha Holman Conwill and Paul Gardullo

Foreword by Eric Foner

Preface by Spencer R. Crew

Contributions by

Kimberlé Williams Crenshaw, Mary Elliott, Candra Flanagan,
Katherine Franke, Thavolia Glymph, Hasan Kwame Jeffries,
Kathleen M. Kendrick, and Kidada E. Williams

**In Association with the National Museum of
African American History and Culture**

AMISTAD
— 35 —

NATIONAL MUSEUM
of AFRICAN AMERICAN
HISTORY & CULTURE
Smithsonian

An Imprint of HarperCollinsPublishers

HarperCollins books may be purchased for educational, business, or sales promotional use. For information, please email the Special Markets Department at SPsales@harpercollins.com.

FIRST EDITION

National Museum of African American History and Culture
Director: Kevin Young
Director Emeritus: Spencer R. Crew
Deputy Director: Kinshasha Holman Conwill
Publications Team: Candra Flanagan, Paul Gardullo, Kathleen M. Kendrick, Danielle Lancaster, Jaye Linnen, and Douglas Remley
Captions by Kathleen M. Kendrick

Produced by Smithsonian Books
Director: Carolyn Gleason
Senior Editor: Jaime Schwender
Assistant Editor: Julie Huggins
Designed by Gary Tooth / Empire Design Studio
Edited by Karen D. Taylor

Library of Congress Cataloging-in-Publication Data is available upon request.

ISBN 978-0-06-316064-4

21 22 23 24 25   LSC   10 9 8 7 6 5 4 3 2 1

Endsheets: The Shackle Broken— by the Genius of Freedom, 1874. The central vignette of this lithograph depicts Rep. Robert B. Elliott delivering a speech in Congress in support of the Civil Rights Act.

Page 1: Portrait of a US soldier with his wife and daughters, ca. 1865.

Page 2: *The Freedmen's Bureau,* 1868. This *Harper's Weekly* illustration by A. R. Waud depicts the Freedmen's Bureau as a peacekeeping force standing between hostile groups of white and Black Southerners.

The question now is, Do you mean to make good to us the promises in your constitution?

—FREDERICK DOUGLASS, speech at Republican National Convention, 1876

CONTENTS

FOREWORD

Eric Foner

OVER A CENTURY AND A HALF after the end of the Civil War, the Reconstruction era that followed that conflict remains a critical turning point in the history of American democracy. During Reconstruction, the nation's laws and Constitution were rewritten to guarantee the basic rights of the former slaves, and biracial governments came to power throughout the defeated Confederacy. These governments created the South's first public school systems, began the process of rebuilding the Southern economy, and sought to protect the civil and political rights of all their constituents.

During this era, the United States tried to come to terms with the consequences of the Civil War—the most important being the preservation of the nation-state and the destruction of the institution of slavery. Reconstruction was a time period—generally dated

Portrait of a woman wearing a US flag, ca. 1865. For African Americans the end of slavery raised hopes that the nation's founding promises of liberty, justice, and equality would apply to all citizens, regardless of race.

1865–77—and a historical process that does not have a clear, fixed end: One might say that in our country, we are still trying to work out the consequences of the end of slavery. In that sense, Reconstruction never ended. Its relevance to the present is highlighted by demands for racial justice that continue to reverberate throughout our society. Issues that roil American politics today—the definition of citizenship and voting rights, the relative powers of the national and state governments, the relationship between political and economic democracy, the proper response to terrorism, racial bias in the criminal justice system—all of these are Reconstruction questions.

Yet, despite its significance, the Reconstruction era has long been misunderstood. For much of the past century, historians portrayed it as a time of corruption and misgovernment—the lowest point in the saga of American democracy. According to this view, Radical Republicans in Congress, bent on punishing defeated Confederates, established corrupt, Southern governments based on the votes of freed African Americans, who were supposedly unfit to exercise democratic rights. This portrayal, which received scholarly expression in the early twentieth-century works of William Dunning and his students at Columbia University, provided an intellectual justification for the system of segregation and disenfranchisement that followed Reconstruction, and for the depredations of the Ku Klux Klan and other violent organizations bent on restoring and maintaining white supremacy. Any effort to restore the rights of Southern Blacks, these writers suggested, would lead to a repeat of the alleged horrors of Reconstruction. As late as 1944, Gunnar Myrdal noted in his influential work, *An American Dilemma*, that when pressed about the Black condition, white Southerners "will regularly bring forward the horrors of the Reconstruction governments and of 'Black domination.'"

Today, having abandoned the racism on which the old view of Reconstruction was predicated, most historians see Reconstruction as a laudable effort to build an interracial democracy on the ashes of slavery. But the old view retains a remarkable hold on the popular imagination, including the pernicious idea that expanding the rights

Portrait of a US soldier, ca. 1865. Approximately 200,000 Black soldiers and sailors fought for freedom during the Civil War. Black veterans asserted that their loyalty and sacrifice earned them the right to full citizenship.

and powers of Blacks constitutes a punishment to whites. For that reason alone, this book is especially welcome. The essays in this volume represent an ongoing effort to reevaluate the Reconstruction era and to reclaim its unrealized potential for achieving racial justice.

Among Reconstruction's most tangible legacies are the three constitutional amendments (see Appendix A on page 200 for transcript) ratified between 1865 and 1870. The Thirteenth Amendment irrevocably abolished slavery throughout the United States. The Fourteenth constitutionalized the principles of birthright citizenship and equality before the law regardless of race. The Fifteenth sought to guarantee the right to vote for Black men throughout the reunited nation. All three empowered Congress to enforce their provisions, radically shifting the balance of power from the states to the nation, ensuring that Reconstruction would be an ongoing process.

The amendments had flaws. The Thirteenth allowed involuntary servitude to continue for people convicted of crime, inadvertently opening the door to the subsequent creation of an enormous system of convict labor. The Fourteenth mandated that a state's number of Congressional representatives would be reduced if it barred groups of men from voting (a provision that was never enforced), but imposed no penalty if it disenfranchised women. The Fifteenth allowed states to limit citizens' right to vote for reasons other than race. Nonetheless, the amendments should be seen not simply as changes to an existing structure, but as a second American founding, which created a fundamentally new Constitution. Taken together, as George William Curtis, the editor of *Harper's Weekly*, wrote at the time, they transformed a government "for white men" into one "for mankind." They laid the foundation for a remarkable, democratic experiment in which, for the first time in our history, Black men throughout the nation were allowed to exercise the right to vote in large numbers, and to hold public offices ranging from members of Congress to state legislators and local officials.

Reconstruction also made possible the consolidation of Black families, so often divided by sale during slavery, and the

This commemorative copy of the Thirteenth Amendment, signed by President Abraham Lincoln, was presented to prominent Republican Schuyler Colfax, Speaker of the House of Representatives, who helped secure the amendment's passage in January 1865.

Thirty-eighth

Congress of the United States of America, at the second session, begun
and held at the City of Washington, on Monday the fifth day of December,
one thousand eight hundred and sixty-four.

A Resolution

submitting to the legislatures of the several States a proposition to amend the
Constitution of the United States.

Resolved by the Senate and House of Representatives of the United States of America
in Congress assembled, (two-thirds of both Houses concurring,) That the following article be proposed to the legislatures of the several States as an amendment to the
constitution of the United States, which, when ratified by three-fourths of said legislatures, shall be valid to all intents and purposes as a part of the said Constitution
namely:

Article XIII.

Section 1. Neither slavery nor involuntary servitude, except as a punishment
for crime whereof the party shall have been duly convicted, shall exist within the
United States, or any place subject to their jurisdiction.

Section 2. Congress shall have power to enforce this article by appropriate legislation

Schuyler Colfax,
Speaker of the House of Representatives

I certify that this Resolution
originated in the Senate

J. W. Forney
Secretary.

H Hamlin
Vice President of the United States,
and President of the Senate

Approved. February 1. 1865.

Abraham Lincoln

Souls to the Polls rally, Miami, Florida, November 1, 2020. A new generation of advocacy often galvanized in Black churches echoes the Reconstruction drive for equal voting rights. Restrictive voting measures passed after the 2020 elections, which include voter ID requirements and limits on early voting, disproportionately impact African Americans and other minorities.

establishment of the independent Black church as the core institution of the emerging Black community. But the failure to respond to the former slaves' desire for land left most with no choice but to work for their former owners. Yet, despite the failure to provide an economic foundation for the freedom that African Americans had acquired, political and social change was so substantial that it evoked a violent counterrevolution. One by one, the biracial governments fell by the wayside, until by 1877 all the Southern states were under the control of white supremacists. By 1900, with the acquiescence of a conservative Supreme Court, the new constitutional amendments had become dead letters in most of the South. As Frederick Douglass observed shortly before his death, "principles which we all thought to have been firmly and permanently settled" had been "boldly assaulted and overthrown."

One lesson of Reconstruction and its aftermath is that our Constitution is not self-enforcing. Rights can be gained and rights can be taken away, to be fought for another day. The civil rights revolution of the 1960s, which swept away the legal edifice of Jim Crow, was sometimes called the Second Reconstruction. Today, despite an alarming resurgence of white nationalism, we may be on the verge of a Third Reconstruction, which will finally address the deep inequalities in wealth, health, education, and treatment by the police that are the legacies of two-and-a-half centuries of slavery and nearly a century of Jim Crow. As long as the legacy of these eras of inequality continue to plague our society, we can expect Americans to return to Reconstruction and find there new meanings for our fractious and troubled times. However flawed, the era that followed the Civil War can serve as an inspiration for those striving to achieve a more equal, more just society.

● ● ●

PREFACE

Spencer R. Crew

IN HIS 1935 SEMINAL WORK, *Black Reconstruction in America: Toward a History of the Part Which Black Folk Played in the Attempt to Reconstruct Democracy in America, 1860–1880*, W.E.B. Du Bois, a preeminent scholar and an uncompromising critic of racism, sought to reinterpret the Reconstruction era. By offering an African American perspective that highlighted the revolutionary potential of this epoch, his goal was to counter the racially biased interpretations advanced by white scholars who thought that it was a failure.

The exhibition, *Make Good the Promises: Reconstruction and its Legacies*, and this companion volume, seek to parallel Du Bois's perspective, and are informed by an African American purview. This approach is fundamental to the efforts of the National Museum of African American History and Culture. We seek to offer our visitors a different understanding of the evolution of the nation and how African Americans navigated and influenced its development. Reconstruction provides such an opportunity because the United States was forced to reconceptualize the meanings of freedom and citizenship, and to come to terms with the formerly enslaved as citizens. The experiences of the newly freed and previously free African Americans are also guides for the narrative unfolding of the exhibition and this publication.

African Americans were a force that fought for and helped to attain freedom for themselves. These four million emancipated individuals faced an uncertain future full of questions and possibilities. Their hope was that the nation would embrace them as equals. Frederick Douglass stated in an 1865 speech, "What the Black Man Wants," "Give him a chance to stand on his own legs! Let him alone!" From Douglass's vantage point, these minimal acts would make it easier for African Americans to enjoy the same rights as any white citizen.

Unfortunately, this was not the path followed. Instead, especially in the South, barriers constantly were placed in the road to freedom for African Americans. This happened despite the passage of the Thirteenth, Fourteenth, and Fifteenth Amendments, which sought to bring America closer to the principles stated in the Declaration of Independence and expanded in the Constitution. Jim Crow laws enforcing discrimination, the system of sharecropping, the rise of the Ku Klux Klan, and the implementation of convict leasing emerged to limit the rights of African Americans and to intimidate them.

However, this was not the full story because African Americans found ways to carve out spaces for themselves. They reunited with lost relatives and forged new relationships between family members. They created businesses, purchased land, and built their own religious institutions. The Black church served as a fulcrum and engine for moral, spiritual, and civic education from Reconstruction through a full flowering in the Civil Rights Movement, valuing and promoting primary and secondary school education as well as founding institutions of higher learning such as Morehouse, Fisk, Talladega, and Shaw. African Americans actively resisted attempts

Entered according to act of Congress in the year 1872 by Currier & Ives in the Office of the Librarian of Congress at Washington.

ROBERT C. DE LARGE, M.C. of S.Carolina.   JEFFERSON H. LONG, M.C. of Georgia

U.S. Senator H.R. REVELS, of Mississippi   BENJ. S. TURNER, M.C. of Alabama.   JOSIAH T. WALLS, M.C. of Florida   JOSEPH H. RAINY, M.C. of S.Carolina.   R. BROWN ELLIOT, M.C. of S.Carolina.

THE FIRST COLORED SENATOR AND REPRESENTATIVES,

In the 41st and 42nd Congress of the United States.

NEW YORK, PUBLISHED BY CURRIER & IVES, 125 NASSAU STREET.

to restrict their political options as new citizens. They were not always victorious, but the efforts of African Americans during this period are essential to highlight.

As important is the fact that the issues that arose from the Reconstruction era continue to resonate: voting suppression, citizenship, reparations, officially condoned violence, and how best to remember the Civil War still challenge the nation. For that reason, Reconstruction must be understood in its full complexity, because it was a lost opportunity for the country to remake itself. Since then, African Americans have organized, boycotted, and advanced legal challenges, but the NAACP's anti-lynching campaign, the Don't Buy Where You Can't Work economic boycotts, the Civil Rights Movement's voting rights campaigns and sit-ins, and Black Lives Matter marches are testimonies to continuing injustices. Whether the country will ever rise to the promise of equality that is declared in its founding documents is not self-evident. Therefore, *Make Good the Promises* offers lessons that, hopefully, will move the nation forward so it can completely fulfill its promise for all of its citizens.

• • •

The First Colored Senator and Representatives, 1872. *Left to right*: Sen. Hiram Revels (Mississippi), Reps. Benjamin Turner (Alabama), Robert DeLarge (South Carolina), Josiah Walls (Florida), Jefferson Long (Georgia), Joseph Rainey (South Carolina), and Robert Elliott (South Carolina).

MARRIAGE CERTIFICATE

M̲r. *Augustus Johnson* and M̲iss *Malinda Murphy*

Were this *Ninth 9th* day of *July* 1874.

legally joined by me in

MATRIMONY

In Presence of — to which I hereby

Charles Bannister Certify.

Joanna Murphy *Abraham Cole*

L. PRANG & CO. BOSTON

INTRODUCTION

Candra Flanagan, Paul Gardullo, and Kathleen M. Kendrick

IN JANUARY 1867, just over a year after the Thirteenth Amendment had declared an end to slavery in the United States, African American author, lecturer, and activist Frances Ellen Watkins Harper perceived her country at a critical crossroads. The poet who had famously penned "Bury Me in a Free Land," in the 1850s, on the cusp of the Civil War—which African Americans would help transform from a battle to preserve the union into one to end slavery—recognized that while the war was over, the struggle for freedom had only just begun. She stepped before an integrated audience gathered in Philadelphia's National Hall, and provided a vision for what she titled our "National Salvation." "Now slavery, as an institution, has been overthrown, but slavery, as an idea, still lives in the American Republic," Harper exhorted her audience in the city that had birthed American democracy. "And the problem and the duty of the present hour is

Marriage certificate with tintype portraits of Augustus L. Johnson and Malinda Murphy, 1874. During Reconstruction, African American couples who had been denied the right to officially marry during slavery embraced marriage as a civil right and claimed the freedom to define their roles as husbands and wives.

MRS. F. E. W. HARPER

Frances Ellen Watkins Harper, a writer and activist, gave eloquent voice to the hopes and possibilities that Reconstruction represented for African Americans, women, and the nation.

this:—Whether there is strength enough, wisdom enough, and virtue enough in our American nation to lift it out of trouble."

That trouble, Harper noted, was rooted in "distinctions between man and man, on account of his race, color, or descent," the racial prejudices and inequities bequeathed by 250 years of chattel slavery. But rather than be discouraged, Harper insisted, "we have one of the greatest opportunities, one of the sublimest chances that God ever put into the hands of a nation or people." This was the opportunity to remake America without slavery by reconstructing the nation on a basis of true freedom and equality.

The dream of a nation emerging from the wreckage of its most devastating war, with its greatest opportunity and its greatest hope in its own hands, was a profoundly and uniquely African American vision. She powerfully located our national salvation in the quiet dignity, the "greediness for knowledge," the faith, aspiration, industriousness, and passion for equality shaped and shared by the nearly five million Black people then living in America.

Joining Harper in articulating this vision of rebirth and progress were many well-known activists such as Harriet Tubman, Sojourner Truth, and, perhaps most famously, Frederick Douglass, who tied this national project of full freedom and equality to a vision for the world and for all humanity. "There are such things in the world as human rights," Douglass declared in 1869. "They rest upon no conventional foundation, but are eternal, universal and indestructible." He saw the possibilities for America in a modern and expansive way—as a "composite nationality" that was "gathered here from all quarters of the globe" and drew its inspiration from the African American fight for freedom.

Amidst the new waves of immigration to the nation and the expansion of America's interests abroad, African Americans also recognized the global contexts and dimensions of their political and social efforts. They bore witness to the fact that freedom was still sought by many outside of the United States, and believed that the destiny of multiracial democracy and self-determination was one that must be shared across and beyond the nation's borders. For instance, throughout the years of Reconstruction, tens of thousands of Black Americans forged solidarity with the movements for full freedom and abolition in Cuba and Brazil. Prominent activists, including Rev. Henry Highland Garnet, founded the Cuban Anti-Slavery Society in 1872 and petitioned the US government to support the cause to end slavery and colonialism in one of America's nearest neighbors. Though Cuba would not abolish slavery until 1886 and Brazil in 1888, the burgeoning movement to form common cause with international matters of Black freedom and self-determination found increasing resonance within African American communities across the nation.

Given voice and clarity by poets, orators, activists, artists, and politicians, this multifaceted vision of national redemption from the injustices of slavery was shared and made manifest by many thousands more African Americans whose names and memories are too often lost to history. These freedom dreams focused inward—on building and sustaining Black communities and institutions, and ensuring collective safety and autonomy—even as they promised to simultaneously remake American citizenship and equality, potentially providing a new model for the world. Though tempered by deep doubt, real anxiety, and practical challenge, African Americans saw true change as palpably within reach during the era known as Reconstruction.

TWO MONTHS after Frances Harper delivered her lecture on national salvation in Philadelphia, Congress passed the First Reconstruction Act, placing the former Confederate states under military rule until they drafted new state constitutions granting voting rights to Black men. The Reconstruction Acts also required Southern states to ratify the Fourteenth Amendment, which established birthright citizenship and equal protection under the laws for all Americans. The Fifteenth Amendment, ratified in 1870, extended the protection of voting rights to Black men nationwide. These amendments, more democratic in scope than any in history, rewrote core tenets of the Constitution. By empowering the federal government to extend and protect civil rights for all citizens regardless of race, the amendments seemed to be the fertile ground upon which newly sown seeds of liberation, if persistently tended, could transform the nation from a slave republic into a multiracial democracy.

The Reconstruction Amendments acknowledged what African Americans already understood: Emancipation was only the first step to full and equal citizenship. To secure their rights and defend their freedom, they needed to construct political power, amass economic wealth, build community, and foster spiritual well-being. African Americans desired to reframe the body politic and to redeem the nation's soul, but their acts of reconstruction also proceeded in the most commonplace and intimate aspects of daily life, personally and communally. Black people embraced freedom by searching for and reuniting their families following brutal separations experienced during enslavement. They officiated and celebrated marriages, claimed new names, and created new institutions for worship, mutual support, and learning—including schools at all levels that would come to model a national system of public education. They sought ownership of land and fair compensation for their labor, and when they could not attain their goals by staying in the South they set out for new places like Kansas, Oklahoma, and South Dakota. Formerly enslaved Black Americans also petitioned the government for pensions and demanded financial compensation for generations of stolen labor and lost wealth. Above all, they insisted upon the opportunity to truly define and determine their own lives, free from white interference.

As Congressional Reconstruction removed racial barriers to the ballot box and political office throughout the South, Black men and women claimed these spaces to define and defend a new vision

RE-CONSTRUCTION,
OR "A WHITE MAN'S GOVERNMENT".

of American democracy, based on racial equality and justice, even if fundamentally incomplete in matters of gender. Black men registered to vote in mass numbers and served as delegates to state constitutional conventions, where they helped craft new state constitutions that guaranteed civil rights and public education to all. They also won elections: Between 1865 and 1876, more than 1,500 African Americans held public office in Southern state and local governments. They served as state senators and representatives, lieutenant governors, city council members, sheriffs, justices of the peace, superintendents of education, and more. And, for the first time in history, African American men served as the nation's lawmakers. The election of twenty-two Black senators and representatives to the US Congress between 1870 and 1901 marked, perhaps, the most visible and dramatic example of African American political gains and the building of Black political power during Reconstruction.

Re-construction, or 'A White Man's Government,' 1868. In this political cartoon mocking Southern Democrats who opposed Black civil rights, a Black man clasping the "Tree of Liberty" extends a hand to a drowning white man who refuses to be saved.

Chain gang working on the railroad at Swannanoa Cut, North Carolina, ca. 1885. The convict labor and lease system perpetuated a form of forced labor akin to slavery under the cover of the Thirteenth Amendment's exception clause.

But advancing the promise of full freedom was thwarted by hardship, terror, violence, and white backlash. After the Confederacy lost the Civil War and slavery was abolished, white Southerners continued to uphold white supremacy as the basis for reconstructing Southern society. These self-described Redeemers used terror, racist propaganda, and political malfeasance to defeat the Republicans, who supported African American civil rights, and ultimately regained political control of the South. In hostile response to the Reconstruction Amendments and the first real exercises of Black power, states and communities across the American South—with the tacit and often explicit support from the federal government—began to construct political and legal systems designed to disenfranchise, police, and criminalize Black freedom, a practice that would come to be known as Jim Crow.

The long shadow of slavery also entwined itself through a system of extralegal practices bent on the surveillance, exploitation, and destruction of Black bodies and lives. Racial terror was reorganized and inflicted through vigilante groups such as the Ku Klux Klan and the Red Shirts, and through various forms of anti-Black violence, from lynchings and massacres to social codes that encouraged Black degradation. Some of the first major outbreaks of racial violence following the Civil War took place in Southern cities such as New Orleans and Memphis, where mobs of white civilians and police attacked and sometimes destroyed African American communities. In the years and decades that followed, such instances of heinous racial violence were repeated both with increasing alacrity and systematic routineness in towns and cities across the nation, including Clinton, Mississippi; Colfax, Louisiana; Hamburg, South Carolina; Wilmington, North Carolina; Atlanta, Georgia; St. Louis, Missouri; Washington, DC; Chicago, Illinois; Elaine, Arkansas; Rosewood, Florida; and Tulsa, Oklahoma. These mass demonstrations of organized white violence and destruction of Black lives and property continued with little recourse or reproach well into the middle decades of the twentieth century.

Fissures were found in the laws as well. The Thirteenth Amendment, which abolished slavery, contained a clause that allowed for its legal continuation as a punishment for crimes. In a modern reconstruction of enslavement, Southern states enacted the system of convict labor and leasing, which criminalized Black freedom in order to secure the control of Black labor. Laws promoted arresting African Americans for minor offenses such as vagrancy, walking on the grass, expectorating on streets or sidewalks, or sleeping in train stations. Men and women convicted of such crimes were imprisoned without due process, disenfranchised, and leased by local authorities to railroads, mines, factories, plantations, and private homes as forced workers. The results were devastating. Once one was brought into the system it was nearly impossible to get out. Convicts built railroads, graded roads, constructed factories, made turpentine, and grew and harvested cotton, timber, and other extractive crops. By the 1880s, convict leasing had become a major source of labor in Southern states, trapping thousands in a system of brutally inhumane working conditions and high death rates. In an exposé on convict labor in the late nineteenth century, the *Cleveland Gazette* reported "the wretched creature is actually a slave, as much in 1883 as in 1860, only that he is worked by the State instead of an individual, and is watched by armed soldiers instead of overseers."

Portrait of Frederick Douglass, 1878. In urging the nation to "make good to us the promises in your constitution," Douglass sounded a call for equality and justice that would continue to echo long after Reconstruction.

White supremacy, however, was not merely a Southern phenomenon made manifest through the terror of violence and convict leasing. It was a nationally held creed, one that persisted and perpetuated itself as a racial caste system of "separate but equal" that was born and enacted through practice and law. It drove the expansion of American political and economic interests throughout the American West and overseas, especially in Central America, the Caribbean, and the Pacific, justifying the subjugation and exploitation of people based on a construct of racial hierarchy that placed white Anglo-Saxons at the top. While the United States had abolished slavery, the structure of racism that had created and supported it remained in place, providing a blueprint for new forms of suppression and opposition to Black liberation on national and global scales. These connections were not lost on African Americans. In an "Address to the Nations of the World" at the first Pan-African Congress in 1900, the young Black social scientist W.E.B. Du Bois—who would go on to illuminate the intersecting struggles of race, class, and democracy in his groundbreaking work *Black Reconstruction in America*—prophesied that "the problem of the Twentieth century is the problem of the colour-line."

Twenty-five years earlier, Frederick Douglass recognized and lamented the rising tide of white supremacy and anti-Black violence as a threat to the freedom that African Americans envisioned for themselves, the nation, and, for some, the globe. During the year of the nation's centennial, at the 1876 Republican National Convention, Douglass saw the continuities with slavery sinking their roots into law, practice, and custom. Despite the ratification of the Reconstruction Amendments that pledged to remake the nation into a multiracial democracy and protect the freedom and civil rights of

African Americans, the promise of these laws alone meant nothing if the nation was not willing to defend and enforce them. "Oh! You freed us! You emancipated us! I thank you for it," Douglass rebuked his fellow Republicans.

> *But what is your emancipation?—what is your enfranchise-ment? What does it all amount to, if the Black man, after having been made free by the letter of your law, is unable to exercise that freedom, and, after having been freed from the slave-holder's lash, he is to be subject to the slaveholder's shot-gun?*

In concluding, Douglass left no doubt as to what was at stake for African Americans and for the future of the nation: "The question now is, Do you mean to make good to us the promises in your constitution?"

Portrait of Oscar J. Dunn, lieutenant governor of Louisiana and one of the first African Americans elected to statewide executive office, ca. 1868. Between 1865 and 1876, more than 1,500 African American men held public office in Southern state and local governments.

THIS TELLING OF RECONSTRUCTION'S history, one seen through the African American lens, is long overdue. The revolutionary changes to American democracy brought by the collective acts of Black people claiming and demanding full freedom resulted in a wave of political, social, and educational prog-ress too long erased from our schoolbooks, unseen in our museums, unremembered in our historic sites, and misrepresented in popular culture. The real struggles, aspirations, and achievements of African Americans during Reconstruction were replaced by a host of mythologies focused on failure and bolstered by violence, stereotype, and institutionalized racism. Reconstruction and the long retrenchment following are deeply relevant to our lives today and demand to be reclaimed and understood as both a period and a process, in order to begin to make good those promises fashioned and then refused by the nation.

The founding vision for the National Museum of African American History and Culture was conceived by Black Civil War veterans in 1915, fifty years after the start of Reconstruction. As African Americans' central role in reshaping the nation was being distorted and erased on a scale never before seen in popular and political culture, the Black soldiers who had fought for freedom and equality under the US flag sought to build a museum in the nation's capital to ensure that their sacrifices were not in vain, and their visions were not forgotten. The same year, the motion picture, *The Birth of a Nation*, premiered to mass acclaim, including praise from President Woodrow Wilson, and inspired a refounding of the Ku Klux Klan. Also, a memorial to Confederate veterans had been dedicated in Arlington National Cemetery, and hundreds more monuments to the Lost Cause were rising on public squares and courthouse lawns across the country. Beyond Hollywood filmmakers and Confederate-heritage promoters, the white supremacist view of the Civil War and Reconstruction was also embraced and perpetuated by prominent historians across the nation's most prestigious universities, such as William Dunning of Columbia University.

Central to the Museum's mission is to remember, retell, and recenter the African American perspective for the benefit of all Americans. Because transformative efforts around race and reenvisioning American history are written into the Museum's DNA, reclaiming Reconstruction is part of our ongoing institutional ethos: The Museum reclaims Reconstruction in its work with the Freedmen's Bureau Transcription Project, a widespread effort at democratizing history that uses crowdsourced transcribing to make hundreds of thousands of Bureau records that document the African American postwar experience accessible to family historians and scholars alike. Reconstruction is reclaimed through the Museum's activities that bring programs and resources to educators, families, students, and the general public that create brave spaces where race and racism, and their legacies of struggles for freedom, are more openly explored and discussed. Reconstruction is reclaimed in curatorial efforts with communities and organizations to collect, preserve, and help interpret the precious material culture of the totality of Black lives, depicting joy, delight, and diversity as well as pain and sorrow.

Reclaiming this history also means engaging in conversations around historical and contemporary incidents of racial violence, and movements for reparations and restorative justice. It means respectfully and urgently working in communities to collect history, such as in Baltimore and Ferguson in the uprisings after the deaths of Freddie Gray and Michael Brown. It means uniting with families, like Trayvon Martin's, in order to collect, protect, and serve as a proper home for objects related to his life and his death, alongside so many others who've entrusted the Museum with their stories and treasures, making sure that we are stewarding this history and their memories truthfully and with deep respect in hope of making change. It means reckoning with national systems of institutional racism, such as the fact that African Americans are imprisoned at six times the rate of white Americans. Therefore, collecting and preserving materials large and small that illuminate the convict labor and leasing system and its connection to the wider history of race and mass incarceration is imperative—particularly for prisons founded on former slave plantations, such as the nation's largest state penitentiary in Angola, Louisiana.

While reclaiming Reconstruction has multiple meanings for the Museum, the most immediate and direct way that we urge a reclamation of this vital period in African American and American history is through this volume and companion exhibition, *Make Good the Promises: Reconstruction and Its Legacies*. The essays in this book expound upon five themes that frame intersecting legacies of Reconstruction—liberation, violence, repair, place, and belief.

Historian Thavolia Glymph's essay "Reconstructing America" grounds readers in the period of the 1860s through the 1890s, providing a vital reframing of Civil War and Reconstruction history told through an African American lens and showing how African American freedom dreams were envisioned, made manifest, and ultimately thwarted. Kimberlé Williams Crenshaw, scholar of critical race theory, charts Reconstruction's "Legacies of Liberation" by provocatively using the lens of women's history to explore the need for a double recovery of gender and race in order to more deeply understand the meanings and intersections of human rights and liberation, inclusive of and beyond the legal and political spheres. "Legacies of Violence" are evoked by historian Kidada E. Williams, coeditor of the influential *Charleston Syllabus*, whose essay gives voice to victims of racial violence. Williams demands that we pay closer attention to the continuing impact of racial violence on the lives of victims and their families and reminds us that anti-Black violence is one of our most persistent national legacies. Legal scholar Katherine Franke recovers "Legacies of Repair" by tracing the long history of movements for reparations and elucidating the connection between present strategies for reparations with those from the 1860s and '70s. In so doing, she asks us to deepen our understanding of the language of repair that is philosophical as well as practical and meaningful to our past and to each other. "Legacies of Place" by Mary Elliott, Museum curator of American slavery, maps the history of a uniquely important place shaped by slavery and freedom. Elliott's deep and personal reading of the history and legacies of race on Edisto Island, South Carolina, reminds us that we need to pay close attention to the power of places no matter how small or large, because they offer a profound connection to our past, our sense of ourselves, our collective identity, and to how we might take hold of and, perhaps, overcome that past. Civil rights historian Hasan Kwame Jeffries's "Legacies of Belief" raises the Black legacy of Reconstruction that has been purposefully erased from popular memory. Jeffries frames the divergent legacies of white supremacy and Black liberation to help us think about the ways the distortion of history, crafted through the myth of the Lost Cause, still structures our public discourse. More importantly, he encourages us to envision how an alternative narrative built upon a history of Black education and truth telling is ready to be reclaimed.

These essays provide tools meant to measure history's impact on our present and to help readers comprehend the unmet promise of making a more equal, just, and free America. Collectively, the

Black Lives Matter demonstration in Washington, DC, June 4, 2020, in response to the murder of George Floyd by Minneapolis police. Protests across the nation throughout June were estimated to be the largest mass movement in US history.

essays demand that we look to the past as a wellspring for liberation today. They also challenge us to uncover and work to illuminate a set of histories that have been minimized, erased, or refused. The essays urge us to engage in the ongoing practice of racial reckoning, asking how we can expect true reconciliation and repair in a society, that generation after generation, keeps revisiting the same histories and examples of violence and injustice, without addressing, respecting, and remedying the pain and wrong done. Finally, they focus on history and belief. Not just upon what is lost, destroyed, or forgotten, but what is projected onto the past and hoped for in the future; what is written into people's hearts and minds—from stone monuments and other features on the landscape, to the books, records, and keepsakes in our schools, courthouses, churches, and homes, to our bodies and our prayers.

The authors of this volume assess the promise, value, and necessity of developing together new narratives that embrace full freedom despite the great challenges of doing so. In telling stories of a people's hope, faith, pain, heartbreak, and struggle, the authors insist that we remember individuals' lives like Susie Jackson, Hawkins Wilson, George Floyd, Warren and Jane Jones, John and Amanda Childers, Ida B. Wells, Recy Taylor, Arlene Estevez, Rev. Clementa Pinckney, and more, in order to address the unfulfilled promises of Reconstruction.

Reclaiming these histories and meeting these promises and the dreams of freedom that animate them is our shared purpose in a nation and a world still seeking social, racial, and political justice and repair.

• • •

Black Lives Matter demonstration in Berlin, Germany, June 6, 2020. Thousands of protests held in cities on all continents around the world demonstrated the global resonance and solidarity of the Black Lives Matter movement across races, cultures, and nations.

RECONSTRUCTING
AMERICA
AN OVERVIEW

Thavolia Glymph

Family standing in front of
former slave quarters on the
Hermitage Plantation near
Savannah, Georgia, ca. 1900.
After emancipation, millions
of formerly enslaved women,
men, and children continued
to live in the American South,
many on the same lands that
their families had worked for
generations. Their quest to
secure their rights and
construct new lives as free
people would shape the era
known as Reconstruction.

ON OCTOBER 12, 1868, at the age of thirty-eight, Henry Moore registered to vote for the first time in his life, in one of the first elections held in the Reconstruction era. By signing the Register of Voters of the Parish of Pointe Coupee, Louisiana, he exercised his right to vote under the terms of the Reconstruction Acts of 1867. The Fifteenth Amendment, which granted African American men the right to vote by making it unconstitutional to deny that right on the basis of race, color, or previous condition of servitude (though not on the basis of sex), was still two years away when Moore and tens of thousands of other Black men, some who were in their nineties, registered in 1868. Most signed the voting rolls with an X that marked their illiteracy on the pages of the registry but also their new status as voters and citizens of the United States. Their journey—part of a centuries-long fight for freedom, citizenship, and the vote that was protracted, uneven, and violent—brings the story of emancipation and Reconstruction to a human scale. Their journey also helps us to remember the central role that individual African Americans played in the struggle, as well as the visions of freedom they had for themselves, their communities, and the nation. Those visions were not widely shared by most Americans who did not envision an end to slavery in their lifetime or that the formerly enslaved would be raised to the status of citizens.

ABRAHAM LINCOLN would lead the nation through America's most deadly war—a war that led to that consequential moment in Pointe Coupee—but unlike most white Americans, he thought hard about the institution of slavery. In 1858, he worried aloud about the deepening crisis between the Northern free states and Southern slave states. It would end, he stated, in the United States becoming "*all* one thing or *all* the other," a nation where slavery was permitted everywhere in its borders or where it was permitted nowhere. Either way, he told his fellow Republicans when accepting the Illinois Republican Party's nomination for the US Senate, the United States would endure. The test of that proposition would come sooner than Lincoln could have anticipated. He addressed the race for the Senate, but two years later, he was elected president of the United States.

On December 20, 1860, South Carolina declared its independence from the United States. In January 1861, delegates meeting in state conventions in Mississippi, Florida, Alabama, Georgia, and Louisiana adopted similar ordinances of secession, followed by Texas on February 1. Three days later, delegates from these seven states met in Montgomery, Alabama, and formed a Provisional Congress of the Confederate States of America, an unabashedly and explicitly proslavery nation-state project. They would be joined by Virginia, Arkansas, North Carolina, and Tennessee in April through June of 1861.

When Lincoln took office on March 4, 1861, seven Southern states had already passed ordinances of secession. He addressed them directly in his first inaugural address. His main message to them was that secession was quite unnecessary, that "the acces-sion of a Republican Administration" did not represent a danger to "their property and their peace and personal security." He objected to the expansion of slavery, like most white Northerners. Represen-tative Thaddeus Stevens of Pennsylvania, for example, had argued in 1850, "Confine this malady within its present limits, surround it by a cordon of free men . . . and in less than twenty-five years, every slaveholding State in this Union will have on its statute books a law for the gradual and final extinction of Slavery." Lincoln was not, however, an abolitionist. On this point, he was explicit, stating that he had "no purpose, directly or indirectly, to interfere with the institution of slavery in the States where it exists," and reiterating his belief that every state had the right "to order and control its own domestic institutions according to its own judgment exclusively," echoing the view of many Republicans and the Republican Party platform. Lincoln was not only keen to address the insurrectionist states, but he also wanted to prevent the four border states of Dela-ware, Maryland, Kentucky, and Missouri from joining the Southern states in rebellion. Slavery was legal in these border states, but it was less central to their economies than it was in the Lower South slave states. Moreover, Lincoln recognized the critical importance of their strategic location, manufacturing capacity, and sizeable population to the Northern war effort. As a result, the border states played a major role in the political and military considerations of the federal government for most of the war.

The president also signaled his eagerness to appease the South with his support of Article 13 (Joint Resolution No. 80). Lincoln sent the article to the states for ratification less than two weeks following his inauguration. It was one of more than two hundred resolutions respecting slavery, including fifty-seven resolutions calling for constitutional amendments, proposed by Congress between Janu-ary 14 and March 2, 1861, that aimed to resolve the secession crisis. It denied Congress the power to abolish or interfere with slavery in any way including by constitutional amendment, in perpetuity. Lincoln made clear that he had "no objection to its being made express,

Bombardment of Fort Sumter by the Batteries of the Confederate States, April 13, 1861. This illustration from *Harper's Weekly* depicts the second day of the thirty-four-hour Confederate attack on the US Army garrison in Charleston Harbor. On April 14, federal troops evacuated, and the Confederate flag was raised over the fort.

and irrevocable." The war intervened before the bill could be fully considered for ratification by most of the states. If it had been ratified, Article 13 would have become the thirteenth amendment to the Constitution. Lincoln saw his support of the bill as another way to demonstrate to the South that he had no intention of interfering with or abolishing slavery where it existed, which he hoped would also appease the Upper South border states.

Lincoln had been in office for a month when insurrectionary forces attacked Fort Sumter, a federal arsenal in the Charleston Harbor, on April 12, 1861. Despite congressional efforts at compromise and despite Lincoln's assurances to white Southerners, war came, and the newly formed Confederate States of America announced in its constitution of March 11, 1861, the centrality of slavery to its mission.

On April 9, 1865, after four years of war, Robert E. Lee surrendered the Army of Northern Virginia to Ulysses S. Grant at Appomattox Court House, Virginia. The defeat of Lee's army effectively ended the Civil War and the South's bid to establish a pro-slavery nation. An estimated 750,000 men had died in the line of duty, as well as an untold number of civilians. For Lincoln, Northern victory had proved, as he stated in his first inaugural address, that the "Union of these States is perpetual." It remained to be determined what kind of union it would be during the war. That would be the work of Reconstruction.

WHEN WAR CAME, white Northerners prepared to fight for the Union, believing, or so they said, that the Civil War had nothing to do with Black people or their right to freedom. Black people insisted, to the contrary, that the war had everything to do with them. Acting on that belief, hundreds of thousands of enslaved women, men, and children left plantations and farms and sought refuge within the lines of the US military in the South, asserting their vision of what the war should stand for. Enlisting as soldiers, nurses, laborers, and spies, they became part of what W.E.B. Du Bois called "the general strike," and Steven Hahn, "the greatest slave rebellion in modern history." Northern soldiers and commanders were often surprised to find enslaved people citing federal legislation that offered them the protection of federal military forces. Along the Mississippi River, naval commanders encountered people with knowledge of the Confiscation Acts, which freed people enslaved by men and women at war against the US. No one called the enslaved to strike but themselves. By 1865, their actions had fueled a transformation in the Northern war aims to include emancipation.

Support for Black freedom as a war aim did not necessarily translate into support for a political vision that saw Black people as equal citizens. For the duration of the war, the vast majority of white Northerners remained committed primarily to a war for unification rather than for Black freedom. Slavery no longer legally existed in most of the North, but prejudice against free Black people remained pervasive. By 1838, for example, free Black people had lost the right to vote in Pennsylvania and New Jersey, and tax or literacy clauses limited their ability to vote in the states of Massachusetts, Rhode Island, Delaware, and Connecticut. In the Midwestern states, so-called Black laws or Black codes restricted the rights of Black people. They required Black residents to post bonds to remain in the states, denied them the right to serve on juries, and disenfranchised Black men. Anti-Black prejudice surfaced during the war in opposition to allowing Black men to serve as soldiers in the US Army and to Black migration to the North except when recruited as domestic servants or farm laborers. The idea that enslaved people could aid the cause of the United States by fighting the Confederacy from inside, behind enemy lines, gained few adherents.

In the North and South, however, the mass self-emancipation exercised during the Civil War forced a new reckoning as Black people took control of their labor power and took the fight to the Confederacy long before the federal government authorized them to do so.

The transformation of the Civil War to a war to free the enslaved, as well as preserve the US nation-state, would redefine the meaning of freedom and citizenship in the United States and place Black people in conversation with federal authorities about military and political strategy. Black people's individual and collective acts of freedom-making contributed to the growing clarity in the North about their potential as allies. Black people's agency also factored into Congressional decisions to pass legislation that sought to remove them as enemy assets, thereby supporting eventual freedom.

From the beginning of the war to the end, bills and resolutions passed by Congress only gradually came to recognize Black people as other than property. Rather, they attached such labels as "captives of war," "fugitives from labor," and "contrabands of war" to them. These labels, couched in the language of property rights, blunted the revolutionary changes underway and encouraged Northerners to imagine Black people as a different species of human beings. This, in turn, made it easier to pretend that a war about slavery was really about the constitutionality of secession. Further, it helped Northerners to imagine that in a war about slavery, the enslaved would have nothing to say.

The First Confiscation Act, formally known as "An Act to confiscate Property used for Insurrectionary Purposes" and passed

Freed children with their teachers, Beaufort, South Carolina, ca. 1862. Along with land, formerly enslaved African Americans sought education as a key to determining their own lives and futures. Many gained their first access to education through schools established by the Port Royal Experiment, a partnership between Northern missionary organizations and the federal government to aid freed people on the US-occupied Sea Islands.

by Congress on August 5, 1861, was the first of the measures regarding enslaved people, and it reflected these issues. By authorizing the confiscation of property used in support of the insurrection, it sought to undermine the Confederacy's capacity to wage war. The act designated enslaved people as property eligible for confiscation, if put to work by slaveholders in support of the Confederacy. Enslaved men forced to build fortifications or entrenchments for Confederate armies fell into this category as did men put to work in navy yards or on ships. Under this act, slaveholders "forfeited" their claims to the enslaved laborers. Confiscating the enslaved was not, however, an act of emancipation. Neither was the Article of War approved by Congress on March 13, 1862, that prohibited soldiers and officers from returning people who made it to their lines—"fugitives from service or labor" in the language of the act—to slavery. Articles of War govern the conduct of military forces. This article addressed conduct that turned US soldiers into slave catchers and sellers of human beings. But what of the forfeited persons—were they free and, if not, under whose authority did they remain enslaved? The federal government did not say, nor did it articulate a plan to emancipate them. By summer, that had changed.

On July 17, 1862, Congress passed an amended Militia Act. Like previous militia acts, it provided statutory authorization for the president to call out the militia to suppress rebellion or repel invasion. In the past it had applied to white men, but the 1862 act applied to all men regardless of race, and allowed enslaved men to serve as military laborers. In return for digging ditches, building fortifications, and performing other labor, they and their mothers, wives, and children would be freed, but only if the person enslaving them was part of or supported the insurrection. These terms did not apply to enslaved men and women in the four border states where slaveholders who had not joined the rebellion were considered loyal. It was not until March 3, 1865, that Congress provided a legislative path to freedom for the wives and children of Black soldiers who belonged to loyal slaveholders from the border states, leading to a surge of enlistments by Black men. This gave added motivation to men like William Jones, who ran away with his wife on Saturday, March 11, 1865, eight days after Congress passed the resolution "to encourage Enlistments" by freeing the wives and children of Black soldiers who belonged to loyal slaveholders from border states like Kentucky. He testified before a notary public at Camp Nelson, Kentucky, the largest recruiting center for African American troops during the Civil War, saying, "[I] Desir[ed] to enlist and thus free my wife and serve the Government during the balance of my days."

Also passed on July 17, 1862, the Second Confiscation Act authorized the seizure, as "captives of war," of enslaved people claimed by men and women "engaged in rebellion against the government of the United States, or who shall in any way give aid or comfort thereto" and made them "forever free." The act encompassed enslaved people who fled to the lines of the US Army or the ships of the US Navy, captured by Union forces, or found in any place occupied by US military forces. The Second Confiscation Act also forbade federal soldiers from impeding any effort by the enslaved to escape slavery and, importantly, it provided for the recruitment and enlistment of African American soldiers. This act moved the federal government one step closer to full emancipation but again exempted loyal slaveholders from its provisions.

The Militia Act and the Confiscation Acts left the actual, practical work of emancipation to enslaved people. The vast majority of those who gained their freedom during the war freed themselves. African Americans persisted in their determination, moving steadily and in increasingly larger numbers into the military lines of the US Army and onto the ships of the US Navy. Still, the federal government persisted in its refusal to grant freedom outright without qualification and failed to adequately protect those who made it to its lines.

Congressional timidity was also on view in the joint resolution passed on April 10, 1862, offering financial assistance—"to compensate for the inconveniences, public and private, produced by such change of system"—to any state in rebellion against the United States if it agreed to adopt gradual emancipation. By "change of system," Congress meant the destruction of slavery and the adoption of a free labor system, even if it meant that the government would enter the market as purchasers of enslaved people.

The Constitution did not give Congress or the president the power to act against slavery in the states, but it could ban slavery in the District of Columbia and the territories. On April 16, 1862, nine months before he issued the Emancipation Proclamation, Lincoln signed the act ending slavery in Washington, DC, in the only act of compensated emancipation in the United States. The government paid loyal slaveholders up to $300 for each person emancipated. The claims commission would approve more than 930 petitions granting freedom to some 3,000 people. The act also authorized an appropriation of $100,000 to be used by any of the people emancipated by this act who volunteered to immigrate to Haiti or Liberia. None chose to do so.

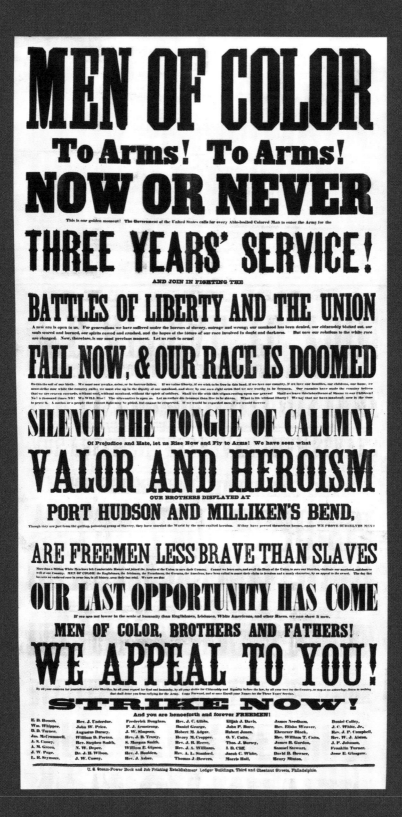

Congress had managed to avoid using the words slave and freedom. The First Confiscation Act, the Article of War of 1862, and the District of Columbia Emancipation Act all avoided using the word slave, substituting euphemisms such as "person held to labor or service."

The Emancipation Proclamation, issued by Lincoln on January 1, 1863, is the most famous of the acts and presidential orders from the war. Explaining his decision to issue the Emancipation Proclamation, Lincoln wrote that it was "warranted by the Constitution, upon military necessity," but also as "an act of justice," and used the occasion to mark the moral distance he had personally traveled. "My whole soul is in it," he stated. The Emancipation Proclamation freed "all persons held as slaves within said designated States, and parts of States" in rebellion against the United States. Yet, despite calling on the executive branch of the government and the War Department to "recognize and maintain the freedom" of Black people, the act did not authorize any particular resources to ensure that their freedom was maintained except at the direction of individual commanders. It announced no national program of emancipation. This meant that Black people would not only have to take steps to free themselves, but also, in the words of Lincoln, "make their actual freedom" and maintain it amidst a war. To free themselves, they would still have to take their fight to the states in rebellion. Acting on their own authority, African Americans played a key role in the military victory of the North.

The proclamation's provision for the enlistment of Black soldiers had an immediate impact: while the US Army was not ordered to become an army of liberation, the presence of Black soldiers helped make it one. Most white Americans remained skeptical that Black men could be made into a fighting force despite all manner of evidence to the contrary—from slave revolts to Black soldiers' service in the Revolutionary War and other conflicts. White Americans argued that Black men lacked courage, would not fight their former masters, could not understand such military matters as battle formation, and that whites would not serve beside or lead

This eight-foot-tall broadside, printed in Philadelphia in June 1863, rallied African American men to enlist in the US Army to prove their valor and patriotism and to fight for the cause of liberty, citizenship, and equality before the law. The signers included Frederick Douglass, whose impassioned speeches and writings galvanized the recruitment effort, along with other African American political and religious leaders, including Octavius Catto and William Whipper.

Emancipation, 1865. In this print celebrating the end of the Civil War, illustrator Thomas Nast presented contrasting views of life for African Americans during and after slavery. In place of brutal overseers and the auction block, the coming of freedom would mean sending children to school, receiving wages for one's labor, and providing a safe and loving home for one's family.

them. These judgments initially kept Black regiments from being assigned to combat duty and were used to justify unequal pay and assigning Black soldiers to manual labor such as digging ditches and building fortifications, breastworks, and log roads. Indeed, United States and Confederate soldiers both came to depend on the labor of Black people on the battlefields and on the home front. Soldiers on both sides ate food grown and cooked by enslaved people and benefitted from the work of Black women nurses and other hospital workers. All came to understand that every enslaved person who ran away from a plantation, farm, or Confederate military camp hurt the ability of the Confederacy to maintain its soldiers in the field and feed and clothe its people at home.

Black people turned the narrow but important paths that legislation carved out into multilane highways that culminated in the Thirteenth, Fourteenth, and Fifteenth Amendments. Before the war ended, Congress passed the Thirteenth Amendment on January 31, 1865. It made slavery and involuntary servitude unconstitutional "except as a punishment for crime whereof the party shall have been duly convicted." Ratified on December 6, 1865, it ended the equivocation over whether the United States would remain an empire of slavery after the war regardless of which side won. It recognized that the nation could not easily reverse the freedom that Black people, including 200,000 Black soldiers and sailors, had fought for not just over the four long and bloody years of the Civil War but over the long history of the nation.

WITH THE DEATH OF President Abraham Lincoln from an assassin's bullet on April 15, 1865, Vice President Andrew Johnson succeeded him. Like Lincoln, Johnson came from humble beginnings and rose to great heights with little formal education. Born in poverty in 1808 in North Carolina, he moved to Tennessee where he became a small slaveholder and politician and served in the Tennessee House of Representatives, and as governor and US Senator before Lincoln appointed him military governor of Tennessee. He was the only senator from a Confederate state to remain loyal to the United States. Largely for this reason, Lincoln chose him as his running mate in 1864.

President Johnson proved to be an enemy of Black freedom despite giving some indication in his first months in office that he would support Black suffrage and punish the leaders of the Confederacy whom he called traitors. Johnson soon changed course and pushed for restoration of the Southern states to full political status that included Congressional representation and fully functioning civil courts and state governments. On May 29, shortly after taking office, he issued his reconstruction plan, which was in line with Lincoln's released in 1863. Both offered a lenient process for the restoration of the Southern states to full political rights. Johnson's plan offered the restoration of property rights and general amnesty to anyone who took an oath of future loyalty, excluding high-ranking Confederate officials and white Southerners with wealth of more than $20,000. Those who exceeded the financial threshold were required to petition Johnson personally. Under Johnson's plan, the former states of the Confederacy were also required to ratify the Thirteenth Amendment and repudiate Confederate war debts. By the end of 1865, all the states that had been in rebellion had established new state governments and all but two had ratified the Thirteenth Amendment. (Texas did so in 1870 and Mississippi in 1995.) Johnson prepared to accept Southern states back into the Union, on an equal basis with all other states, and hoped to have the process completed by the time Congress came back into session in December. Johnson's contempt for Black people was also increasingly evident. Freedom, he told a delegation of Black ministers on May 11, 1865, "simply means liberty to work and enjoy the products of your own hands. This is the correct definition of freedom, in the most extensive sense of the term."

On October 11, 1865, President Johnson granted paroles and pardons to former leaders of the Confederate states and government and the most powerful men and women who had supported the insurrection, signaling his complicity with white Southerners' determination to maintain white supremacy. By May 4, 1866, Johnson had pardoned some 7,000 Southerners whose wealth exceeded $20,000 and 12,652 by June, averaging 200 per day between May 4 and June 5, 1866. By July 1867, 949 persons had received pardons in the state of Mississippi alone, 800 of whom possessed wealth over $20,000. Using his pardon power and the provisions of his reconstruction plan, Johnson ensured that few leaders of the insurrection would face any significant punishment for having committed treason.

Under Johnson's reconstruction plan, the South sent representatives and senators to Congress in December 1865. The delegation was dominated by men who had taken up arms against the United States or held political office in Confederate local, state, or national government. To some Republicans, the composition of the delegation signified a brazen lack of repentance, which was also made apparent by provisions in new Southern state constitutions and

legislation that maintained white supremacy. White Southerners accepted the Thirteenth Amendment to regain their political power, but they never intended to share it with Black people. A century later, into the 1960s, white supremacists' hold on power would increase in scope and violence, in both spectacular and quotidian ways.

Johnson's control of Reconstruction would soon come to an end. The midterm elections of 1866 returned a two-thirds Republican majority in both houses of Congress. But Republicans were not of one accord on the question of how to reinstate the insurrectionary states to the United States. Radical Republicans—members of the Republican party committed to abolition and the equal treatment of freed Blacks—wanted a robust plan that would protect Black freedom, grant Black men the vote, and block men who had led the rebellion from elected office. The reluctance of newly reestablished Southern state governments to abolish slavery and grant Black men the right to vote—what one white Mississippian called "the odious principle of negro suffrage"—worried them. The passage of Black codes and the

On July 30, 1866, white police officers attacked a gathering of freedmen outside the Louisiana Constitutional Convention, which was meeting to revise the state's laws to include suffrage and civil rights for African Americans. At least thirty-four people were killed. Republicans blamed President Andrew Johnson for the violence, citing his vetoes of civil rights legislation and support for ex-Confederates. This 1867 painting by Thomas Nast depicts "King Andy" overseeing the New Orleans massacre.

election of former Confederate office holders to state and national office were further disconcerting signs of an unreconstructed white South, a South unwilling to accept Black freedom and equality.

Beginning with Mississippi, Alabama, and Louisiana in late 1865, Southern legislatures passed Black codes that aimed to maintain white supremacy and a subservient Black labor force. The codes reflected the confidence of white Southerners that they could act with impunity and as if slavery had not been declared unconstitutional. In early 1866, Florida, Virginia, Georgia, North Carolina, Texas, Tennessee, and Arkansas passed similar codes.

Some codes banned assemblies of Black people day or night, unless they possessed documents proving that they were gainfully employed, which typically meant employed by a white person. If they did not have these documents, they could be classified as vagrants and subject to imprisonment or fines. The codes also fined and threatened with imprisonment white people who assembled with "freedmen, free Negroes, or mulattoes on terms of equality" or lived in adultery with Black people. In Mississippi, the code empowered every white person to arrest any Black person they found in violation. Quitting a job before the expiration of one's contract could result in the forfeiture of all wages for the year up to that time. The codes also punished "seditious speech" and forbade Black people from owning arms, ammunition, dirks, or bowie knives unless they were a member of the army or licensed by a county board of police. The codes recognized emancipation and the right of Black people to sue in court and marry but denied them full parental rights. Black parents could easily be declared unfit and have their children stripped from them under vagrancy and apprenticeship provisions of the codes. Black men could be arrested for failure to pay child support and, if unable to give bond, be "obliged to sell themselves or their services" for one to seven years. In Mississippi, Black people could not rent property in cities or towns. In addition to laws restricting their freedom, Black people found themselves subject to the arbitrary dictates of white Southerners against which there was little recourse.

Into this breach stepped agents of the Bureau of Refugees, Freedmen, and Abandoned Lands. The Freedmen's Bureau, as it was popularly known, was established within the War Department by Congress in March 1865 with a mission to provide assistance to white Unionists in the South and oversee and assist the formerly enslaved in the transition to freedom. The Bureau was charged with ensuring adherence to constitutional changes, such as citizenship and voting rights. John Berry, of Alexandria, Virginia, was a prime example of the need for the Bureau's services. In the summer of 1865, he returned from the war and went to get his wife and six children, but the man who enslaved his family refused to give them up, telling Berry that "the war was not over yet." Like many white Southerners, he took offense at Black freedom and Black men like Berry who had taken up arms against the Confederacy.

In Brentsville, Virginia, a Black military veteran turned to the Bureau when he was attacked by a white man for appearing "impudent," meaning the white man felt that the veteran was not behaving in a servile manner. In North Carolina, Samuel Harrington sought help from the Bureau to free his wife from John Dongel who still held her "as a slave." Jane Stewart sought out the Bureau to secure the release of her two children from Dickinson Dowd. In South Carolina, Hagar Barnwell turned to the Bureau after her employer tied her up and threatened to kill her when she tried to leave after refusing to do work that was not in her contract. In Sampson County, North Carolina, a Bureau agent reported the sale of two Black men by local authorities.

The Freedmen's Bureau never had enough money or personnel, and some of its agents proved to be more sympathetic to the concerns of white Southerners than Black people, but it did important work. Some 900 agents, scattered across the South, documented thousands of cases of violence against Black people and other infractions of the law. It helped Black people legalize marriages from the slavery era and new marriages and adjudicated labor contracts. It issued millions of rations to poor Black and white people. It staffed forty-six hospitals and supported the establishment of Black colleges, including

THE NATIONAL COLORED CONVENTION IN SESSION AT WASHINGTON, D. C.—SKETCHED BY THEO. R. DAVIS.—[SEE FIRST PAGE.]

Held in Washington, DC, in January 1869, the National Convention of the Colored Men of America called upon Congress to secure suffrage and other equal citizenship rights for African Americans. Miss H. C. Johnson of Pennsylvania won the right to be admitted as the sole female delegate to the conference. Many other women also attended, as this *Harper's Weekly* illustration *The National Colored Convention in Session at Washington, D.C.* shows.

Fisk University, Howard University, and Hampton Institute, as well as public schools, concluding its educational work in 1870. Originally planned to last for one year, Congress renewed the Bureau in 1866 over President Johnson's veto, and eventually defunded it in 1872.

While Mississippi, Alabama, and Louisiana were passing laws to restrict the freedom of Black people, Black men met in state conventions to chart a different path forward. For example, the Colored People's Convention of the State of South Carolina met at Zion Church in Charleston for five days in late November 1865. The delegates drafted several statements of purpose including one that read, "We ask only for *even handed justice*." They issued a "Declaration of Rights and Wrongs," citing the injustice and inhumanity of slavery and declaring the "right to be free in our persons, and the right of personal security and protection against injuries to our bodies or good name." They condemned the Black codes and called for a "code of laws for the government of all, regardless of color." Black delegates to the state constitutional conventions placed these demands into the new state constitution adopted April 16, 1868, which outlawed "distinction on account of race or color" and decreed that "all classes of citizens shall enjoy equally all common, public, legal and political privileges."

Thus, Reconstruction began with Black people having to contend with Black codes, economic intimidation and exploitation, and the violence perpetrated by individual white people and terrorist organizations such as the Ku Klux Klan, the White Brotherhood, the Knights of the White Camelia, the Rifle Clubs and Red Shirts, and the White Leagues of Louisiana.

Founded in Pulaski, Tennessee, in 1866, the Klan became the most infamous of the domestic terrorist organizations that arose after the war. From 1866 to 1871, its members burned and destroyed Black homes, farms, and businesses; murdered hundreds, including Black and white Republican officeholders and teachers; raped Black women; and stole an inestimable amount of property in land, crops, food and household goods, and animals from African American people. Klan violence also targeted Black men who attempted to vote, serve on juries, or hold office.

Dismayed by the actions of President Johnson and white Southerners, Congress, led by the Radical Republicans, moved to take full control of Reconstruction beginning with the Civil Rights Act of 1866. It declared that "all persons born in the United States and not subject to any foreign power, excluding Indians not taxed, are hereby declared to be citizens of the United States; and such citizens, of every race and color, without regard to any previous condition of slavery or involuntary servitude, except as a punishment for crime whereof the party shall have been duly convicted," thus establishing birthright citizenship. It also conveyed to every person regardless of race or color certain basic civil rights: the right to make and enforce contracts, to sue, be parties to suits, and testify in court; to inherit, purchase, and sell real and personal property; and the right to equal benefit of all laws pertaining to the security

While the Ku Klux Klan was founded in Tennessee and operated primarily in the South during Reconstruction, support for its terrorist activities and white supremacist agenda reached far beyond the former Confederate states. This photograph of ten young white men, wearing not hoods, but hats labeled "K.K.K." and posing with a skull and crossbones, was taken in Watertown, New York, ca. 1870.

of person and property enjoyed by white citizens. It marked the first time Congress had legislated on civil rights—and the first significant law to override a presidential veto.

With the passage of the Fourteenth Amendment on June 13, 1866, and its ratification on July 9, 1868, birthright citizenship, initially codified in the Civil Rights Act of 1866, became a constitutionally guaranteed right. All persons born in the United States, regardless of "race or color" or "previous condition of slavery or involuntary servitude" were declared citizens of the United States. The Fourteenth Amendment also made it unconstitutional for any state to "deprive any person of life, liberty, or property without due process of law" or to deny "equal protection of the laws." It provided for but did not require Black male suffrage. Although states that deprived African American men of the vote would have their representation in Congress reduced proportionately, with the exception of Tennessee, every Southern and border state that considered adoption of the amendment between October 1866 and January 1867—North Carolina, South Carolina, Georgia, Virginia,

Texas, Kentucky, Delaware, Maryland, and Louisiana—rejected it. The Civil Rights Act of 1866 and the Fourteenth Amendment were direct responses to the Black codes and formed a critical part of the radical program to establish Black freedom, ensure the civil rights of all regardless of race, and suppress ongoing acts of insurrection by white Southerners. Still, it was increasingly clear to the Republican Congress that even more was necessary to reconstruct the South and curb the violence and general outlawry. To this end, Congress passed four Reconstruction Acts that outlined the terms and concrete process for the establishment of new state governments.

The First Reconstruction Act of March 2, 1867, required the establishment of new governments in Virginia, North Carolina, South Carolina, Georgia, Mississippi, Alabama, Louisiana, Florida, Texas, and Arkansas. It also required Black male suffrage, ratification of the Fourteenth Amendment, and laws that provided for equal rights for all citizens. The act divided the ten states into five military districts under a commanding general of the army. Each of these military commanders were empowered to protect life and property and oversee the creation of new governments.

The Second Reconstruction Act of March 23, 1867, clarified the process for determining who was eligible to vote and thus making up the election rolls, as well as other voting procedures. The Third Reconstruction Act of July 19, 1867, reiterated that the only legal state governments and officeholders were those recognized by the US government. The Fourth Reconstruction Act, passed March 11, 1868, set the conditions for ratification of the new state constitutions. As the states regained statehood, the military commanders of the five districts turned power over civil affairs to them.

The Reconstruction Acts that allowed Black men to vote for representatives to state constitutional conventions were limited in scope of action and did not have the authority of a constitutional amendment, which meant that the acts were of no use to Black men in the North. In the North and the South, Black people understood that without the vote, they could not effectively advocate for and protect themselves. Congress too concluded that the kind of political

On March 31, 1870, one day after the Fifteenth Amendment was declared ratified, Thomas Mundy Peterson (*left*) voted in a local election in Perth Amboy, New Jersey, a state which had barred Black men from voting since 1807. In 1884, the citizens of Perth Amboy presented him with this gold medal (*right*), which features a bust of Abraham Lincoln on the front and an inscription on the back honoring Peterson as "the first colored voter in the US under the provisions of the Fifteenth Amendment." He is wearing the medal in this portrait.

and social change needed in the South would not happen if Black men were denied the vote.

Black Northerners had to contend with Democrats who opposed Black male suffrage like Indiana Senator Thomas Hendricks. "I say we are not of the same race; we are so different that we ought not to compose one political community," Hendricks stated. Iowa governor William M. Stone, however, supported Black male suffrage. Citing Black people's "unwavering fidelity to the Union" and Black soldiers' courage on the battlefield, he pushed for the elimination of Black codes from the state's books and supported striking the word *white* from Iowa's voting requirements. In 1868, Iowa became the first state outside of New England to grant Black men the right to vote.

Some Americans who opposed the Fifteenth Amendment saw it as part of a radical conspiracy to promote Black equality and increase the power of the federal government at the expense of the states. A Republican senator from California was concerned that the amendment would allow the Chinese to vote, a move he argued would be fatal to the party in the state. Some white women suffragists like Elizabeth Cady Stanton opposed it because it ignored the claims of women for the franchise. Stanton also believed it rewarded men she considered undeserving. The Fifteenth Amendment, she wrote, favored the ignorant "Patrick and Sambo and Hans and Ung Tung" over deserving white women like "Lydia Maria Child, Lucretia Mott, or Fanny Kemble" and, of course, herself. Stanton stood opposed to Black women abolitionist activists like Frances Ellen Watkins Harper, who accused white women of paying too little attention to race. A cofounder and national vice president of the National Association of Colored Women's Clubs, Harper was a major voice in the movement for women's suffrage but also supported the Fifteenth Amendment.

There were others who believed the Fifteenth Amendment did not go far enough. Some Radical Republicans, for instance, wanted to see an amendment that outlawed tying the right to vote to property ownership, poll taxes, educational requirements, and religious beliefs. Opposition to a broadly construed amendment arose not only from anti-Black prejudice but concern that it would undermine state laws that placed property and other kinds of restrictions on the franchise.

The Fifteenth Amendment ultimately was passed and ratified in 1870. President Ulysses S. Grant applauded it as "the most important event that has occurred since the nation came into life." In Northern and Southern cities, towns, and hamlets, and on plantations, steamboats, and roadways, Black people and their white allies celebrated its passage. Massive celebrations were held in major American cities like New York. In Baltimore, more than 10,000 people participated in a parade and more than 20,000 people came out to watch it. In Philadelphia, the celebration lasted more than five hours, featuring speeches and a parade that included a wagon with a printing press that reproduced copies of the amendment for distribution along the parade route.

Pages 60-61: The central scene of this chromolithograph depicts the massive parade held in Baltimore, Maryland, on May 19, 1870, to celebrate the ratification of the Fifteenth Amendment. Vignettes around the border show African Americans enjoying the liberties and rights of equal citizenship, including voting and political representation, land ownership, military service, religious worship, marriage, and education.

COLFAX

CONSTITUTION
OF THE
UNITED STATES.

THE RIGHT OF CITIZENS OF THE UNITED STATES TO VOTE
SHALL NOT BE DENIED OR ABRIDGED BY THE U.S. OR ANY
STATE ON ACCOUNT OF RACE COLOR OR CONDITION OF
SERVITUDE.
— 15th AMENDMENT.

WE TILL OUR OWN FIELDS.

WE WILL PROTECT OUR COUNTRY AS IT DEFENDS OUR RIGHTS.

JOHN BROWN

FREEDOM UNITES THE FAMILY CIRCLE.

T MAY 19th 1870.

OUR REPRESENTATIVE IN THE NATIONAL LEGISLATURE.

THE HOLY ORDINANCES OF RELIGION ARE FREE.

From an original Design by James C. Beard.

AMENDMENT.

9th 1870.

WHILE FILLED WITH CHALLENGES, Reconstruction was also a hopeful time for Black people. Black men were elected to national, state, and local office, and helped draft, and often spearheaded, progressive legislation and new state constitutions. African Americans traveled long distances to gather family members torn apart before the war and placed advertisements in newspapers seeking long-lost family members. With limited resources, they built schools, hired teachers, paid their salaries, and purchased supplies, sometimes forming associations to raise the funds to do this work. They boarded teachers in their homes without charge. Adults joined children and grandchildren in the school room to receive an education. Children taught the alphabet to their parents at night in their cabins.

While the vast majority would not experience drastic changes in their basic way of life and remained poor, poorly sheltered, and without adequate medical care, freedom meant the enjoyment of a life greatly different from slavery. Black babies were no longer born enslaved. Black people would no longer be bought and sold on the auction block or in an enslaver's yard or parlor. Black people could buy land, sometimes forming cooperatives or "work groups" and "companies" to accomplish their goals. They saw the property that they had accumulated under slavery recognized when they took claims for property confiscated by US armies during the Civil War to the Southern Claims Commission. Created by Congress in 1871, the Southern Claims Commission received and considered claims submitted by Southern Unionists—men and women in the South who had remained loyal to the United States during the war—for reimbursement.

Bit by bit, Black people worked to transform slave cabins into free homes. Black women domestic workers demanded contracts that allowed them to work from home, spend more time with their families, and tend cash or food crops. Freedom brought an end to the pass system that had required Black people to carry papers giving them permission to be on the roads and riverways or about the neighborhoods. In freedom, the associational life of Black people strengthened. They not only built public schools but built and supported colleges and banks. Masonic lodges and other fraternal and benevolent organizations came out of the shadows alongside political organizations like the Union League.

Small but important transformations in Black people's lives helped sustain larger visions of what freedom should entail, even as white Americans erected new barriers. Freedom of mobility, for example, was constrained by law and by the power of white people to do as they pleased. Through the use of fraudulent contracts and informal cabals, former slaveholders prevented Black people from seeking better contracts. A group of former slaveholders in Virginia, for example, resolved to bind themselves to not hire or rent land or a house to any Black person "freed by Federal authority" who did not have a written pass or recommendation from "his former master or employer." Black people were forced into peonage or involuntary labor in payment for fraudulently assessed debts for food, clothing, and other necessities furnished by the landlord before the crop was harvested. The Anti-Peonage Act of 1867 made debt peonage unlawful but did little to end the systemic robbery of Black people's wages, debt bondage, and potential to accumulate wealth all exacerbated by unending violence.

Congress finally acted in response to reports of outrages against Black people with a series of Enforcement Acts in 1870 and 1871 (the Force Acts) that outlawed the Klan and other white terrorist organizations. The acts also empowered the president to use military force and relevant enforcement provisions from the Civil Rights Act of 1866 and the Fourteenth Amendment to place national elections under federal control, and empowered federal judges and US marshals to supervise polling places in order to protect African Americans. A Senate investigative committee held hearings in North Carolina and took testimony from Black and white Southerners. It presented the damning findings in the "Report on the Alleged Outrages in the Southern States by the Select Committee of the Senate." The 1872 "Report of the Joint Committee to Inquire into the Condition of Affairs in the Late Insurrectionary States" was

Born in New Jersey and trained as a missionary, Tunis Campbell worked for the Freedmen's Bureau and later served as a Georgia state senator during Reconstruction. In 1865 he purchased 1,250 acres at Belle Ville, Georgia, and established the Belle Ville Farmers Association to promote African American land ownership and economic independence.

HARTWELL

equally damning. By 1872, Klan violence had abated but extraordinary violence by armed white mobs and gangs continued, resulting in the murders and massacres of Black people at places like Colfax, Louisiana, and Hamburg, South Carolina.

The strides for equality and the retrenchment toward inequality that encapsulate the larger arc of the story of Reconstruction are most poignantly seen through the lives of African American women and men who strove to make ways for themselves, their communities, and their nation. One such example is Tunis G. Campbell, a Northern-born free Black abolitionist who moved to the South in 1863 to work with freed people on the coast of South Carolina. He remained after the war as a Freedmen's Bureau agent. In 1865 he purchased 1,250 acres at Belle Ville, Georgia, and established an organization to sell land to African Americans when others refused to do so. He was elected justice of the peace in McIntosh County, as a delegate to the state constitutional convention, and state senator, becoming the highest ranking and most powerful Black politician in the state.

Campbell persevered despite intimidation. When white Democrats tried to deny him his seat in the state senate, Campbell recalled the speech he gave in protest, "Upon the question of the eligibility to office I was compelled to stand alone for eight days on the floor of the Senate, contending for the rights of the colored members to hold their seats, and at different times when I was speaking I could see Democratic members, with their hands on the butts of their pistols, with their teeth shut hard together, and using threatening gestures at me." As a member of the legislature, he pushed for equal educational opportunities, integrated jury boxes, and the abolition of imprisonment for debt.

As the 1870s progressed, former Confederates reclaimed the reins of power by passing laws like poll taxes, which greatly reduced the number of Black voters. They targeted places where African Americans had made the most strides, including McIntosh County. In a coup, they removed Campbell from office and replaced him with a white Democrat. They burned his home and poisoned him because of his activism. In 1876, at the age of sixty-three, Campbell was arrested on the trumped-up charge of having improperly arrested a white man when he served as justice of the peace. He was convicted of malfeasance in office and marched chained through the streets of Savannah to a convict labor camp to serve a year's sentence. He returned to the North after his imprisonment, and died in Boston in 1891.

By the time of his death, the time had passed when a Black American like Tunis Campbell could be elected to office or hold substantial political power in the South.

ERIC FONER HAS REFERRED to Reconstruction as the "second revolution" or the "second founding" that was "a stunning and unprecedented experiment in interracial democracy."

Extraordinary change, indeed, did occur. An estimated 1,500 Black men were elected to office during Reconstruction, including two US senators as well as congressmen, justices of the peace, and state legislators. Black legislators helped draft state constitutions that were some of the most progressive in the history of the South. Indictments brought against the Klan under the 1870 Enforcement Act signaled that white supremacists would not be permitted to act with complete impunity.

The constitutional amendments and civil rights laws codified during Reconstruction established the supremacy of the federal government over the states regarding rights and privileges that derived from citizenship. While these changes in the law represented a revolutionary transformation, the experience of freedom often fell short of its promise. By 1875, the newly created Department of Justice (1870) had begun to curtail prosecutions of Klan members under the Enforcement Acts, and many who had been convicted received pardons. Proposals at the state and federal levels to confiscate plantations and redistribute land to the freed people were soundly defeated. Freedmen's Bureau agents reported the unrelenting violence and atrocities, as gangs like the Red Shirts terrorized Black communities.

The 1870s witnessed a shift in the public's opinion and the views of many Republicans about the South and its troubles. The Compromise of 1877 exacerbated the Northern retreat from the South and from the defense of Black freedom. In 1874, Democrats won control of the House of Representatives for the first time since the war. The Compromise of 1877, which resolved the disputed presidential election of 1876, was another bellwether in white Northerners' march away from the problems of the South. In that election, the Democratic candidate, Samuel Tilden, governor of New York, won the popular vote but was one vote shy of the 185 electoral votes he needed to win. Returns from South Carolina, Louisiana, and Florida, which

Spelman College founders Sophia B. Packard and Harriet E. Giles (*standing*) with seminary students, 1886. The first Black colleges and universities in the South were established during Reconstruction, including the Atlanta Baptist Female Seminary (later Spelman College), founded in 1881. Many of the women and men who graduated from these institutions became prominent educators as well as community leaders, organizers, and activists for social justice.

controlled a total of nineteen electoral votes, were disputed along with one electoral vote from Oregon. In this unprecedented situation with no guidance from the Constitution and Democrats controlling the House of Representatives and Republicans controlling the Senate, a bipartisan electoral commission was formed. It gave the Republican candidate, Rutherford B. Hayes, all the contested states, and party leaders met behind closed doors in what became known as the Compromise of 1877, in which Hayes agreed to end federal intervention in the South and place a Southerner in his cabinet. He kept his promise by withdrawing the remaining federal troops in Louisiana and South Carolina. The Democrats pledged to respect the civil rights of African Americans—a pledge they did not keep. For nearly a century, the Democratic Party reversed the gains of the Reconstruction era through violence, intimidation, and laws that imposed segregation and disenfranchised the Black population.

Helping to unravel the gains of Reconstruction were Supreme Court decisions such as the *Slaughterhouse Cases* (1873), which undermined the protections accorded under the privileges and immunities clause of the Fourteenth Amendment. *United States v. Cruikshank* (1876) absolved the perpetrators of the massacres at Colfax, Louisiana. The Fourteenth Amendment, the court said, covered only state action, not acts of discrimination or murder by individuals.

In the Civil Rights Cases of 1883, the Supreme Court declared the Civil Rights Act of 1875, which affirmed the rights of all persons to the enjoyment of transportation, hotels and inns, theaters, and other places of public accommodation and amusement, unconstitutional. The act subjected privately owned places of public accommodation to public regulation but the court disagreed, ruling that the Fourteenth Amendment applied only to the states and did not prohibit discriminatory behavior by private citizens.

In a final blow, *Plessy v. Ferguson* (1896) declared racial segregation constitutional as long as the facilities were equal. In the end, none of the amendments or civil rights acts proved sufficient to overcome racism and new forms of repression and barriers to voting rights that white Southerners erected. Also lost was hope in the possibility of federal protection, which had been a critical innovation of Reconstruction.

The legacies of Reconstruction include the persistence of white supremacy and violence over democracy. Disenfranchisement, lynching, massacre, and loss are also lessons from this history. But Reconstruction is also a story of an effort to remake the nation through constitutional amendments that promised, for the first time, a democracy based neither on race nor class and equal protection and due process of law to all people—ideas that were never previously written into law or the Constitution. African Americans forced the nation to do so. For African Americans, the lessons of both the gains of Reconstruction and retrenchment following would shape struggles for full freedom and equality for more than half a century. Multiple generations of freedom movements spanning the political, economic, social, cultural, and legal spheres ushered in victories—such as the Supreme Court's decision in *Brown v. Board of Education* (1954) and the passing of the Civil Rights Act of 1964 and the Voting Rights Act of 1965. These victories reshaped American life and culture by the time of the 1960s, a moment some have termed a Second Reconstruction. More than fifty years since those landmark events, the legacies of Reconstruction continue to be contested and the freedom movements to ensure equality for all Americans continue to be waged.

• • •

RECONSTRUCTING AMERICA
1861–1896

The traditionally defined time frame for Reconstruction is 1865 to 1877. For this timeline, a broader view is taken to see how struggles over citizenship and national identity developed before, during, and beyond the period. The timeline begins in 1861 with the arrival of formerly enslaved freedom seekers at Fort Monroe, Virginia, and ends in 1896 with the *Plessy v. Ferguson* Supreme Court decision, which made second-class citizenship for African Americans the norm for more than fifty years.

Heroes of the Colored Race. This 1881 chromolithograph features a central portrait of Frederick Douglass flanked by the first Black US senators, Hiram Rhodes Revels and Blanche Kelso Bruce. The corner portraits depict four African Americans elected to the House of Representatives during Reconstruction: Joseph Rainey and Robert Smalls of South Carolina, Charles E. Nash of Louisiana, and John R. Lynch of Mississippi.

1861

MAY 23
First freedom seekers arrive at Fort Monroe in Hampton, VA, prompting Gen. Benjamin Butler's order declaring them "contraband" of war who would not be returned to Confederate slaveholders

JULY 25
Congress passes Crittenden-Johnson Resolution, declaring purpose of the war is to "preserve the Union," not to interfere with "rights or established institutions" (i.e., slavery)

AUGUST 6
Confiscation Act: Based on the US seizure of property used for military purposes, all enslaved people who were forced to fight or work for Confederate services are freed of further obligations to their enslavers

SEPTEMBER
Mary Smith Peake, the first African American teacher hired by the American Missionary Association, begins teaching freedpeople in Hampton, VA, the future site of Hampton University

1862

MARCH
Port Royal Experiment: Program established by Northern abolitionists in US-occupied Sea Islands, SC, to promote education and economic independence for freedpeople

APRIL 16
Emancipation Act: Congress abolishes slavery in the District of Columbia, with monetary compensation to enslavers who claim to support the US; also repeals discriminatory laws restricting the rights of free Black people

May 20
Homestead Act opens up millions of acres of public land for free settlement; prompts migration westward and provides later opportunities for African Americans moving out of the South

JULY 2
Morrill Act (Land Grant College Act) sets aside 30,000 acres of federal lands in each state to create colleges for agricultural and mechanical arts

JULY 17
Second Confiscation Act declares people who are enslaved by rebels to be "forever free" if they come within US Army lines

Militia Act authorizes President Lincoln to enroll African Americans in the US armed forces for "constructing intrenchments, or performing camp service, or any other labor, or any military or naval service for which they may be found competent"

SEPTEMBER 27
L'Union, the first African American newspaper published in the South, is launched in New Orleans, LA

1863

JANUARY 1
Emancipation Proclamation takes effect; US Army begins actively recruiting African American soldiers later in the spring

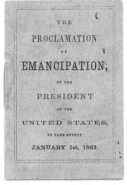

Reading copy of the Emancipation Proclamation, 1862

MAY 5
War Department establishes Freedman's Village in Arlington, VA, on the confiscated plantation of Confederate Gen. Robert E. Lee

JULY 13–16
New York Draft Riots: White working-class mobs, angered by a new federal draft lottery, attack African American homes, businesses, and institutions, including the Colored Orphan Asylum, and kill over 100 people

JULY 18
54th Massachusetts Regiment of US Colored Troops leads assault on Fort Wagner, SC

SEPTEMBER
President Lincoln announces plan to auction 60,000 acres of confiscated lands in South Carolina, reserving 16,000 acres for sale to African American families in 20-acre plots at $1.25 an acre

DECEMBER 8
President Lincoln issues Proclamation of Amnesty and Reconstruction (Ten Percent Plan); requires former Confederates to accept emancipation but does not address issue of rights for formerly enslaved people

---

1864

JANUARY–MARCH
James Walker Hood establishes first AME Zion congregations in the South, at Andrews Chapel in New Bern, NC, and Purvis Chapel in Beaufort, NC

MARCH 1
Rebecca Davis Lee Crumpler is the first African American woman to earn a medical degree

APRIL 12
Fort Pillow, TN, Massacre: Confederate troops under the command of Nathan Bedford Forrest kill an estimated 200 Black US soldiers, most after surrendering

JUNE 15
Congress authorizes equal pay, equipment, arms, and health care for African American US troops

OCTOBER 4–7
National Convention of Colored Men held in Syracuse, NY

1865

JANUARY 16
Gen. William T. Sherman's Special Field Order No. 15 sets aside land in South Carolina and Georgia in 40-acre plots for African American families; origin of term "40 acres and a mule"

MARCH 3
Freedmen's Bureau established; Freedman's Savings Bank and Trust Company incorporated

Congress approves a joint resolution liberating the wives and children of African American US soldiers

MARCH 21
Thousands of freedpeople and US Colored Troops participate in a "Jubilee of Freedom" to celebrate the liberation of Charleston, SC

APRIL 3
US Colored Troops participate in the liberation of Richmond, VA, capital of the Confederacy

APRIL 9
Gen. Robert E. Lee, leader of the Confederate Army of Northern Virginia, surrenders to Gen. Ulysses S. Grant at Appomattox Court House, VA

APRIL 14–15
President Lincoln is assassinated; Vice President Johnson becomes president

MAY 29
President Johnson issues plan for Reconstruction, which pardons Confederates who take a loyalty oath, returns Confederate lands distributed to freedpeople to former owners, and requires states to abolish slavery but does not address civil rights for African Americans

JUNE 19
"Juneteenth": Enslaved African Americans in Galveston, TX, receive news of emancipation

FALL–WINTER
Colored Conventions held in former Confederate states; African American delegates demand civil rights and protest exclusion from state constitutional conventions

NOVEMBER AND DECEMBER
Mississippi and South Carolina enact Black codes restricting the freedom of African Americans and compelling them to work for white planters; other Southern states pass similar legislation in early 1866

DECEMBER 4
Republican majority in Congress refuses to seat newly elected Southern members, many of them former Confederate officials

DECEMBER 18
13th Amendment ratified, abolishing slavery throughout the United States; first of three Reconstruction Amendments to the US Constitution giving Congress new power to define and protect civil rights at the federal level

1866

FEBRUARY 7
A delegation of African American men, including Frederick Douglass, meets with President Johnson to lobby for federal protection of civil rights

APRIL 9
Congress passes Civil Rights Act of 1866 over President Johnson's veto; first national law to establish equal civil rights, regardless of race

MAY 1–3
Memphis massacre: Mobs of white civilians and police attack the Black community; 46 African Americans killed, 75 injured; homes, churches, and schools burned

MAY 10
National Woman's Rights Convention held in New York; Frances Ellen Watkins Harper gives a speech addressing Black and white women, "We are all bound up together"

MAY–JUNE
Ku Klux Klan founded by Confederate veterans in Pulaski, TN

JULY 16
Congress passes bill to extend the Freedmen's Bureau over President Johnson's veto; includes provisions to support land ownership, education, and civil rights protections for freedpeople

JULY 24
Tennessee becomes the first former Confederate state to be readmitted to the US

JULY 30
New Orleans massacre: White Democrats attack a parade of mostly Black Republicans outside Louisiana Constitutional Convention, killing at least 34 and wounding over 130

AUGUST
Representatives of Northern and Western Black Baptists meet to form the Consolidated American Missionary Baptist Convention, the first national Black Baptist association

SEPTEMBER 21
All-Black regiments known as Buffalo Soldiers are commissioned in Fort Leavenworth, KS; these military units mainly serve in the Western US until the early 1900s

OCTOBER 24
Oregon legislature bans marriage between white people and people of African, Chinese, native Hawai'ian, or Native American descent; many states pass similar laws against interracial marriage to restrict citizenship and reinforce white supremacy

FALL
Republicans win midterm elections, retain control of Congress

1867

JANUARY 8
Congress grants suffrage to Black male citizens of the District of Columbia over President Johnson's veto; on January 10, Congress passes Territorial Suffrage Act, allowing African American men in Western territories to vote

JANUARY 10–12
National Equal Rights League Convention of Colored Men held in Washington, DC, to press for voting rights and equal protection under the law for African Americans throughout the country

FEBRUARY 14
Augusta Baptist Institute (future Morehouse College) founded in Georgia

MARCH 2
Howard University charter approved by Congress, Washington, DC

Howard University, late 19th century

MARCH 2
Congress passes the First Reconstruction Act, which places Southern states under military rule until they ratify the 14th Amendment and draft new constitutions granting voting rights to Black men

AUGUST 22
Fisk University incorporated with aid of Freedmen's Bureau, Nashville, TN

OCTOBER
Rev. James H. Holmes becomes the first Black pastor to lead First African Baptist Church of Richmond, VA, since its founding in 1841

DECEMBER
First Southern state constitutional conventions with African American delegates participating are held in Georgia and Virginia

1868

FEBRUARY
Alabama's Reconstruction government establishes the first state-funded public school system in the South, open to all children; by 1870, all Southern states have state-funded public schools

FEBRUARY 24
House of Representatives votes to impeach President Johnson; in May, Senate votes to acquit

APRIL 1
Hampton University founded in Virginia under the auspices of the Freedmen's Bureau

APRIL
Oscar Dunn is elected lieutenant governor of Louisiana, one of the first African Americans elected to statewide executive office

MAY
State of Georgia begins leasing convicts to provide labor for railroad construction; after 1880, convict leasing

system becomes widespread throughout the South

JUNE
Seven more former Confederate states (Arkansas, Florida, North Carolina, South Carolina, Louisiana, Alabama, and Georgia) are readmitted to the US; Georgia's admission status is later revoked after white politicians vote to expel African American members from the state legislature

JULY
Democratic Party nominates Horatio Seymour for president on a white supremacist platform

JULY 6
Congress passes a bill allowing for the Freedmen's Bureau to be discontinued in former Confederate states that have rejoined the US

JULY 9
14th Amendment ratified, granting birthright citizenship and promising due process and equal protection of the laws to all residents of the US

SEPTEMBER 28
Opelousas, LA, massacre: The execution of 27 Black prisoners is followed by a series of attacks on African Americans by white Democrats in St. Landry Parish; an estimated 200–300 people are killed

NOVEMBER 3
Republican Ulysses S. Grant elected president with help from newly enfranchised Southern Black voters

NOVEMBER 3
John Willis Menard of

Louisiana is the first African American elected to US Congress but is not seated due to an election dispute

John Willis Menard, ca. 1868

1869

MARCH 27
South Carolina Land Commission established; state-funded program to purchase plantation land for resale on long-term credit helps hundreds of African American families become landowners before ending in the 1890s

MAY 10
First Transcontinental Railroad completed, making coast-to-coast rail travel possible

OCTOBER
Tennessee and Virginia become the first Southern state governments in which white conservative Democrats (Redeemers) regain control, ousting Republicans

DECEMBER
Colored National Labor Union organized in Washington, DC, led by Isaac Myers of Baltimore, MD

DECEMBER 10
Territory of Wyoming extends voting rights to all women, regardless of race. It is the first time American women are granted full voting rights since 1807, when New Jersey rescinded female suffrage

1870

JANUARY 20
Hiram Rhodes Revels of Mississippi is the first African American elected to the US Senate

JANUARY–JULY
Last of the former Confederate states (Virginia, Mississippi, Texas, and Georgia) are readmitted to the US

FEBRUARY 1
Jonathan Jasper Wright of South Carolina is the first African American elected to a state supreme court

FEBRUARY 3
15th Amendment ratified, stating that a citizen's right to vote cannot be denied "on account of race, color, or previous condition of servitude"; some women's rights activists oppose the law because it does not ban restrictions based on sex

MARCH 26
Tennessee state constitution makes payment of a poll tax a requirement for voting; repealed in 1873; reinstituted in 1890

MAY 25
Congress passes the first of three Enforcement Acts, authorizing the federal government to protect the civil rights of African Americans in response to violence and terrorism by the Ku Klux Klan

JULY 14
Naturalization Act of 1870 allows immigrants of African descent to become US citizens; Asians and other people of color remain excluded until the mid-1900s

OCTOBER 12
Former Confederate Gen. Robert E. Lee dies and becomes a heroic symbol of the Confederacy

DECEMBER 12
Joseph Rainey of South Carolina becomes the first African American to serve in the US House of Representatives

1871

JANUARY 4
Robert H. Wood becomes mayor of Natchez, MS; he is one of the first African Americans elected mayor of a US city

JANUARY 7
William Finch and George Graham become the first African Americans to serve on the Atlanta City Council

MARCH 4
42nd US Congress includes five African American members in the House of Representatives

APRIL 20
Congressional committee organized to investigate Ku Klux Klan violence against African Americans in the South; collects thousands of pages of testimonies; issues report in February 1872

OCTOBER 10
Murder and martyrdom of Octavius V. Catto, a Philadelphia civil rights leader who struggled against racial discrimination in transportation, sports, politics, and society

Octavius V. Catto, ca. 1871

1872

MARCH 21
California Civil Code enacted, includes an 1850 law declaring "all marriages of white persons with negroes or mulattoes are illegal and void"; state supreme court overturns the law in 1948

APRIL 23
Charlotte E. Ray, the first woman to graduate from Howard University's Law Department, is admitted to the bar of the District of Columbia and becomes the first African American woman to practice law in the US

MAY 22
President Grant signs the Amnesty Act, which restores civil rights to most former Confederates

JUNE 30
Freedmen's Bureau is officially abolished

NOVEMBER 5
Republican President Grant wins a second term in the election; number of African Americans elected to state and national political office in the South reaches highest level, will not be matched again until the 1990s

DECEMBER 9
P. B. S. Pinchback of Louisiana becomes the first African American governor in the United States and serves until January 13, 1873

1873

APRIL 13
Colfax, LA, massacre: Armed groups of white men allied with the Democratic Party attack Black Republicans and state militiamen at the Grant Parish courthouse; over 100 African Americans are killed, including 40 prisoners executed after they surrendered

APRIL
US Supreme Court decision in *Slaughterhouse Cases*

limits the civil rights protections of the 14th Amendment; in *Myra Bradwell v. State of Illinois*, the court rules the 14th Amendment does not protect a woman's right to practice law

SEPTEMBER 18
Panic of 1873: Closing of US banking firm Jay Cooke and Company triggers major financial crisis, collapse of railroad and banking industries, widespread unemployment; economic depression lasts until 1879

1874

JANUARY 6
Rep. Robert B. Elliott of South Carolina delivers celebrated speech in Congress advocating for the Civil Rights Act

JUNE 29
Freedman's Savings Bank closes due to mismanagement; thousands of African Americans lose their deposits

NOVEMBER 3
White paramilitary groups allied with the Democratic Party attack African American voters in Barbour County, AL; 7 African Americans are killed and 70 others wounded

NOVEMBER 4
Democrats regain the majority in the US House of Representatives for the first time since 1860

DECEMBER 7
Vicksburg, MS, massacre: White paramilitary groups allied with the Democratic Party attack supporters of Black Republican sheriff Peter Crosby; as many as 75 to 300 African Americans are killed

1875

MARCH 1
Civil Rights Act of 1875 guarantees equal access to public accommodations and public transportation "to citizens of every race and color, regardless of any previous condition of servitude"

MARCH 5
Blanche Kelso Bruce of Mississippi is the second African American to serve in the US Senate and the first elected to a full six-year term

MARCH 23
Tennessee state legislature passes the first "Jim Crow" law legalizing racial discrimination in public places and public transportation

1876

MARCH 27
US Supreme Court rules in *United States v. Cruikshank* that the 14th Amendment does not apply to actions of individual citizens, just to state officials

APRIL 5
Mississippi "Pig Law" makes theft of livestock worth more than $1 a felony; between 1874 and 1882 most Southern states pass similar laws to make more crimes punishable by imprisonment and disqualification from voting, aimed at African Americans

APRIL 14
Freedmen's Memorial, also known as the Emancipation Memorial, funded by contributions from the newly freed, is dedicated in Washington, DC

JUNE 29
Edward Alexander Bouchet is the first African American to receive a PhD from an American university (Yale), and the sixth American to earn a PhD in physics

JULY 4
Centennial of the Declaration of Independence

JULY AND SEPTEMBER
Massacres in Hamburg and Ellenton, SC: White paramilitary groups attack Republican voters in an attempt to secure Democratic control of state government; over 100 African Americans are killed

OCTOBER
Meharry Medical College, the first medical school for African Americans in the South, is founded in Nashville

NOVEMBER 7
US presidential election in dispute: Republican candidate Rutherford B. Hayes and Democratic candidate

Samuel Tilden both claim victory in three Southern states (Florida, Louisiana, and South Carolina); throws country into political turmoil for several months

MARCH
Compromise of 1877: Republican candidate Rutherford B. Hayes becomes president in exchange for recognizing Democratic control of state governments and ending federal intervention in the South; while regarded as the official end of Reconstruction, African Americans continue to vote, serve in office, and assert their rights

JUNE 14
Henry O. Flipper becomes the first African American cadet to graduate from West Point Military Academy

SEPTEMBER 17
Discouraged about prospects in their home state, the first wave of 350 Black settlers from Kentucky arrive in the "Colored Colony" of Nicodemus in western Kansas

DECEMBER
Georgia ratifies a new state constitution that includes a cumulative poll tax as a voting requirement and disenfranchise persons convicted of various crimes, including larceny

APRIL 21
Liberian Exodus Joint Stock Steamship Company sends 206 African American emigrants from South Carolina to West Africa

Liberian ship *Azor*, 1878

MAY 11
Ohio state legislature repeals an 1853 law requiring the establishment of separate public schools for African American children; gives school districts the right to organize segregated schools if "in their judgment it may be for the advantage of the district to do so"

SPRING
Peak of the Exoduster Movement: More than 20,000 African Americans migrating from the South pass through St. Louis, MO, on their way to Kansas and other parts of the Great Plains

NOVEMBER 4
The Readjuster Party, a coalition of Black and white voters, wins control of the Virginia state legislature; implements reforms, including abolishing the poll tax and increasing funding for public schools

APRIL 11
Spelman College (formerly the Atlanta Baptist Female Seminary) founded in Atlanta, GA

JULY
Washerwomen in Atlanta, GA, organize a massive strike for better wages and working conditions; other domestic workers are also inspired to organize

JULY 4
Tuskegee Institute founded in Alabama by Booker T. Washington

JANUARY 21
South Carolina legislature passes the "Eight-Box Law," requiring voters to put ballots into separate boxes labeled with names for each elected office, effectively creating a literacy test for voting

MAY 6
Chinese Exclusion Act signed by President Arthur bans the immigration of nearly all Chinese laborers to the US

1883

JANUARY 1
Chicago Tribune begins publishing annual statistics on lynchings in the United States

JANUARY 22
US Supreme Court decision in *United States v. Harris,* involving a white sheriff prosecuted for the lynching of Black prisoners, rules that federal civil rights enforcement law only applies to state action, not crimes committed by private persons

SOUTHERN HORRORS.
LYNCH LAW
IN ALL
ITS PHASES

Miss IDA B. WELLS.

Price, · · · Fifteen Cents.

Title page of Wells's *Southern Horrors,* 1892

SEPTEMBER 15
Ida B. Wells refuses to give up her seat on a first-class ladies' train car in Memphis, Tennessee, and is dragged off the train; she sues the

railroad company and wins, but the decision is over-turned in 1887

OCTOBER 15
US Supreme Court in the Civil Rights Cases rules the Civil Rights Act of 1875 unconstitutional; allows for discrimination against African Americans by private businesses including hotels, theaters, and transportation companies

NOVEMBER 3
Racial violence breaks out in Danville, VA, before elections, fueled by white conservative backlash against the interracial Read-juster Party rule; Democrats retake control of the Virginia state legislature on a white supremacy platform

1884

SEPTEMBER 23
Judy W. Reed of Washington, DC, is the first African American woman to receive a US patent for an invention, an improved dough kneader. Sarah E. Goode of Chicago, IL, later receives a patent for a folding cabinet bed

1885

FEBRUARY 21
The Washington Monument is officially dedicated, com-

memorating US president George Washington. The construction of the monu-ment, which had been halted due to lack of funds, was reignited in 1876 by the national tide toward sectional unity

1886

SEPTEMBER 4
After 30 years of fighting for his land and people, Apache chief Geronimo surrenders to the US government—a significant turning point in the struggle between Native Americans and the United States

OCTOBER 28
The Statue of Liberty, a gift from the people of France, is dedicated in New York City

DECEMBER 11
Colored Farmers National Alliance and Cooperative Union is organized in Texas to provide economic and political support for African American farmers; chapters are organized across the South, with 1.2 million mem-bers by 1891

1887

FEBRUARY 8
Dawes Act signed into law as part of the federal govern-

ment's goal to "Americanize" Native Americans; effectively breaks up Native American tribes and commandeers land for white settlers

1888

MARCH AND OCTOBER
First banks fully operated by African Americans established: Savings Bank of the Grand Fountain United Order of True Reformers in Richmond, VA, and Capital Savings Bank in Washington, DC. Others include the Mutual Trust Company in Chattanooga, TN (1889), and the Alabama Penny Savings and Loan Company in Birmingham, AL (1890)

1890

JANUARY
National Afro-American League established in Chicago, IL; founded by journalist Timothy Thomas Fortune to organize and advocate for African American civil rights

FEBRUARY 18
The National American Woman Suffrage Association is formed. This organiza-tion played a pivotal role in advocating for women's right to vote, which would not be secured nationwide until 1920 by the 19th Amendment to the Constitution

AUGUST 30
Congress passes the Second Morrill Act, which supports establishment of 18 Black land-grant universities, most in former Confederate states

NOVEMBER 1
Mississippi state constitution requires poll tax and literacy tests for voting; similar voting restrictions aimed at disenfranchise African Americans follow in other Southern states: Arkansas (1892), South Carolina (1895), Louisiana (1898), North Carolina (1900), Alabama (1901), Virginia (1902), and Texas (1902)

DECEMBER 29
Wounded Knee massacre: US soldiers attack a camp of mostly unarmed Lakota Sioux in South Dakota, killing more than 250 men, women, and children

MARCH 3
Immigration Act signed into law, expanding the regulation of who can immigrate to the US; Ellis Island, an immigrant inspection station, opens in 1892 to enforce the act

JULY 4
Populist Party established; political platform focuses on issues of land, the rights of labor, criticism of capitalism, railroads, and banks, and champions silver as the base specie for the US economy

OCTOBER 12
The Pledge of Allegiance is first recited in US public schools

OCTOBER 26
Ida B. Wells publishes *Southern Horrors: Lynch Law in All Its Phases*, reporting on the increasing number of lynchings of African Americans in the South

1893

MAY 1
The World's Columbian Exposition opens in Chicago, IL, and introduces the public to inventions such as the Ferris wheel, Aunt Jemima pancake mix, Quaker Oats, and the first moving walkway. African American leaders boycott the fair after officials refuse to include an exhibit created by the African American community

MAY 3
Financial panic plunges the nation into a four-year economic depression

JULY 12
Historian Frederick Jackson Turner debuts his "Frontier Thesis," in which he declares the US frontier closed and argues that westward expansion was central to the development of American democracy. This view would provide support for new US foreign policies aimed at expanding the nation's territory and influence overseas

NOVEMBER 7
Women in Colorado are given the right to vote

1894

SEPTEMBER 10
The United Daughters of the Confederacy is formed to memorialize Confederate soldiers. They promoted the Lost Cause myth of Confederate history by funding hundreds of Confederate monuments across the South and approving textbooks used in public schools

1895

FEBRUARY 20
Frederick Douglass dies in Washington, DC

JUNE 26
W.E.B. Du Bois becomes the first African American to receive a PhD from Harvard University

SEPTEMBER 18
Booker T. Washington gives his "Atlanta Compromise" speech at the Cotton States and International Exposition, proposing how Black and white Americans could coexist: "In all things purely social we can be as separate as the fingers, yet one as the hand in all things essential to mutual progress"

1896

MAY 18
US Supreme Court ruling in *Plessy v. Ferguson* upholds the constitutionality of state-mandated racial segregation in public accommodations and establishes the "separate but equal" doctrine that will define American life for the next half century

JULY 21
National Association of Colored Women is established in Washington, DC; Mary Church Terrell is elected the organization's president

Mary Church Terrell, ca. 1910

NOVEMBER
George Henry White is elected to Congress as a Representative from North Carolina. After serving two terms (1897–1901), he will be the last African American to serve in Congress until 1929

LEGACIES
OF
LIBERATION

Kimberlé Williams Crenshaw

Walter Jackson holds a framed photograph of his mother, Susie Jackson, two days after she was murdered by a white supremacist at Emanuel AME Church in Charleston, South Carolina, on June 17, 2015. At 87, Jackson was the oldest of the nine church members killed in the attack, which occurred during an evening Bible study meeting. Six of the victims were women.

SUSIE JACKSON WAS BORN into a lineage of a people enslaved by revolutionaries, freed by a Civil War, liberated from an enduring statelessness in the land of their birth, and, later, tragically abandoned on the altar of regional reconciliation. By the time Susie was born, slavery itself had ended some sixty years prior, but its presence could still be touched by the children of Susie's generation, from stories of grandparents who were born into bondage, and from the memories of their children born into what they all had hoped was the dawn of liberty. The shadow of slavery hung over these African Americans born a half century later, anchoring their narrowed possibilities in the segregated worlds they inherited. At best, they were second-class citizens; at worst, they were neither citizens nor human beings, but bodies that could be abused or lynched for sport. Branded by law as a race of "enslavable" people, African Americans were a caste set apart from every other group, precluded from birth to death from leading ordinary lives as citizens of a democratic republic that arose from a war of colonial liberation.

By the time Susie Jackson was born, the sun had long since set on Republican efforts to transform a republic predicated on forced reproduction and stolen labor into a truly multiracial democracy. Reconstruction had been an effort to boldly mobilize law and federal power to advance Black freedom in the same way that law and federal power had been used to inflict Black misery. Armed by constitutional amendments with the right to vote, Black men elected representatives who ruled as equals to whites in biracial democracies throughout the South. But, after just a few years, thousands of Black elected officials and their constituents were forced to relinquish interracial power sharing and to abandon their efforts to build schools, labor cooperatives, and new democratic forms of government. The fruits of citizenship that Black men and women across the South worked so diligently to nurture had blossomed, but they soon withered under the winter of white revolt.

After the violent overthrow of multiracial democracy throughout the South came the lies about Reconstruction—defamatory fabrications about Black political agency that were rehearsed by presidents, pundits, and historians alike. By 1928, Reconstruction's "great moment in the sun" for freed people was widely critiqued as a tragic mistake rather than as a historical period whose promise was violently aborted by racist insurrections.

For African Americans who were left with the empty promise of Reconstruction's grand scheme, the fleeting grasp of freedom seeded liberationist dreams that intermittently broke through the cemented underlife of white supremacist domination. And, for Black people of Susie Jackson's generation, the promise and tragedy of Reconstruction's hopefulness and disappointment were constantly relived throughout their lifelong encounters with America's promise and reality.

Stirrings of freedom's possibility followed by a sobering chaser of racial retrenchment accompanied Susie's trajectory throughout the twentieth century. She was a teenager at the zenith of one of the greatest migrations in American history, as millions of Black people abandoned the South, seeking new possibilities in regions where the stain of slavery was a far more distant memory. She was just about twenty when the post-World War II lynchings of Black servicemen and the unyielding discrimination they faced soured their hopes that a war fought abroad would lift the yoke of oppression at home. She was twenty-six when the Supreme Court breathed new life into the promise of democracy with its groundbreaking decision of *Brown v. Board of Education*, and she was twenty-seven when the mutilated remains of fourteen-year-old Emmett Till, battered beyond recognition by white men ostensibly avenging the honor of a white woman, were displayed in an open casket by Till's mother so the whole world could "see what they did to [her] boy." Susie was thirty-five when Martin Luther King Jr. spoke for millions at the March on Washington in 1963, demanding that the nation fulfill its long overdue promises to African Americans, and she was forty when his voice was silenced by a white supremacist's bullet. Another lifetime passed— forty years after King's heartbreaking assassination—before she witnessed the barrier-shattering election of the first Black president.

As she reached eighty-seven years old, Susie Jackson, a lively and respected elder of Emanuel AME Church, known as Mother Emanuel, in Charleston, South Carolina, had lived nearly nine decades in a nation that had enslaved, tortured, segregated, and repressed her people. Yet by 2015, she had spent seven years witnessing an entirely unthinkable possibility in 1928—a Black family resided at 1600 Pennsylvania Avenue. Susie, no doubt, had reason to believe that she had outlived the ritualistic violence that had terrorized her ancestors and that had reared its head intermittently over the course of her life.

The two-hundred-year-old church she entered on the morning of June 17, 2015, was itself a monument of survival: Razed once by fire and once by earthquake, and twice rebuilt by Black parishioners, Mother Emanuel was a testament to a Black congregation's intergenerational determination to outlive the trials and tribulations of white supremacy. But that fortress of Black strength and pride became a portal for something very different the evening that white supremacy's walking incarnation, embodied in a boyish-looking man barely out of his teens, walked into the open arms of Mother Emanuel. Within an hour, he had murdered the nine people who had welcomed him in prayer and worship. Among the dead were Mother Emanuel's senior pastor and South Carolina State Senator Clementa C. Pinckney. Of all of the victims of his savage rampage, eighty-seven-year-old Susie Jackson was the most brutalized. Dylann Roof riddled her body with eleven bullets, annihilating Jackson along with her fellow worshipers because, in his words, "[Black people] are raping our women and taking over the world."

The enduring horror of the nation's murderous appetite for Black flesh, irrespective of age or gender, was terrifyingly evident in the horrific acts of a Millennial who came of age in the twenty-first century. Possessed by the same bloodlust that snuffed out the freedom dreams of Jackson's elders over a century ago, it carried with it the unique signature of a sexualized terrorism forged in an orgy of anti-Black violence. That this was a continuation of an ideological war against the very idea of Black humanity was confirmed in Roof's embrace of the Stars and Bars, the same flag under which the violent crusade to oppose the abolition of American slavery was waged.

THE FLAG UNDER WHICH Roof's homicidal nationalism rests flew high above the grounds of the South Carolina State House in 2015. It was by special legislation that the Stars and Bars occupied a place of honor on the grounds of the capitol—not as a symbolic gesture honoring South Carolina's secession in the nineteenth century, but in defiance of the Civil Rights Movement in the twentieth century.

Amid the shock and bereavement following the Charleston massacre, Bree Newsome, a Black woman about a decade older than Roof, became determined to dislodge that fixture of white supremacy from its place of pride at the state capitol. Sometime after five thirty in the morning, ten days after the massacre at Mother Emanuel, she cut an arresting image against a cloudy Carolina sky, descending from a thirty-foot flagpole with that symbol of racial

On June 27, 2015, Bree Newsome climbed the flagpole on the grounds of the South Carolina State House and took down the Confederate flag. She represented an interracial group of activists who were moved to respond to the massacre of nine church members at Emanuel AME Church in Charleston.

tyranny firmly in her grasp. Newsome brought the Confederate flag down, disrupting a decades-long stalemate in which the flag had been framed as an immovable embodiment of Southern honor. Officers waiting below promptly arrested her and charged her with defacing monuments on state capitol grounds, an offense punishable by three years in jail. But her defiance became a viral symbol of a reckoning whose time had come.

Newsome's climb was the well-rehearsed, secretly planned, collective action of a small interracial group of activists, executed over several days following the massacre. Even Newsome's immediate family did not know of her plan. She recalls that when the decision was made that she would be the one who would scale the pole, she asked for a day of solitude to meditate, pray, and to put her private affairs in order. She realized that there was a very real possibility that whoever undertook this act might not survive. To learn how to climb the pole, she trained with an experienced climber and practiced climbing at other locations. Acting on her faith and her commitment to liberation, Newsome, inspired and determined, set out to directly dislodge this contemporary homage to white supremacy. In doing so, she embodied the resistant spirit of generations of Black women activists who had come before her. Of her conviction to do so after the Mother Emanuel massacre she stated, "I don't want to live like this. I don't want to live with this kind of indignity."

The Charleston massacre and Newsome's bold act of resistance reflect the unfinished business of Reconstruction. The rise and rationalization of racial violence as a defense of the white family, the white nation, and white rule are historically linked to deliberate efforts on the part of radical, white Southern Redeemers to crush Reconstruction through terror across the South. The violence unleashed did not die once Reconstruction was eliminated—in fact, racial terrorism would extend far beyond its immediate deployment in the nineteenth century.

For far too long, the revisionist history surrounding and deflecting the brutality of Reconstruction's overthrow by white Redeemers has framed Black liberation as a failed experiment, while simultaneously rehabilitating Southern secession as a noble and just cause. Echoes of this ideological defense of slavery and Reconstruction's violent denouement can be heard in contemporary discourses, ranging from policing and mass incarceration to states' rights and voter suppression.

The vibrant, panoramic vision of Reconstruction—the dream of a truly democratic possibility—can be seen in activities that stretch across the venerable heritage of the Black freedom struggle: in the insistence that Black Lives Matter and in the demands to #SayHerName; in marches to demand police accountability and demilitarization in the face of bipartisan enablement; in African Americans' continued insistence on the right to vote despite equally tenacious efforts to suppress Black political participation; and in the brilliant, cross-gendered tradition of Black activism and leadership in the face of life-endangering repercussions.

The continued activism and imagination of African Americans to demand equality and freedom within a republic purportedly dedicated to such ideals is a contradiction that echoes Black women's struggle within that struggle. From Reconstruction until today, Black women have shaped their freedom dreams as Black people and as Black women in particular—making a history that, like Reconstruction writ large, demands recovery today.

Despite the wide terrain of racial struggle, the gendered dimensions of oppression and liberation are often obscured in the most common retellings of Black struggle. For example, Susie Jackson's death at the hands of a racist vigilante hellbent on punishing Black men for rape is almost impossible to fathom within the most common ways of understanding sexualized racism. Roof's homicidal rampage was a contemporary chapter of the grand narrative that framed and justified racial terrorism in terms of the alleged threat of Black men to white womanhood. Absent from the lived histories of these assaults on Black men, and in the broad understanding of how white supremacy has manifested itself, are the realities surrounding the white supremacist violence toward Black women, including lynching and rape.

Bravely called out by Ida B. Wells and a few others, the record of white supremacist terrorism on the lives and bodies of Black women has yet to form into a fully integrated account of white supremacy and Black resistance to it. That an eighty-seven-year-old great-grandmother could be obliterated by a man defending white womanhood against fantasies of Black male aggression demands a reckoning with the particularly gendered ways that Black women have been subjects of widespread physical and sexual abuse, as well as racial terrorism arising in relation to the victimization of their sons, fathers, and brothers.

Similarly, the strained ability to reckon with Black women as objects of racist oppression as well as their continuous role as agents of change was manifest in the troubling ways that some observers read Bree Newsome's courageous climb to remove the Confederate flag. In the aftermath of her ascent, she noted that people were "definitely . . . bothered by seeing a Black woman have that kind of agency." Unable to fathom Newsome as one of a long line of women who directly contested white supremacy, some observers speculated that she was an exotic dancer or a clueless accomplice of a "white daddy." The sidelining of Black women's resistance and freedom dreams throughout history is not new—and that process of erasure suppresses the lineage of struggle out of which they have come.

Despite this erasure, Newsome's early morning climb was a contemporary enactment of Black women's freedom-dreaming that has been handed down through the centuries. It reflects a struggle for liberation against a social order that would banish Black women to permanent subservience twice over—as Black people unfit for citizenship, and as a lesser kind of this lesser kind. This conjoined struggle is part of the obscured vision that the recovery of Reconstruction's lessons cannot afford to leave unaddressed.

RECONSTRUCTION'S POSSIBILITIES were manifest in the countless ways that Black freedpeople took up the tasks of undoing the very conditions of their "enslavability," challenging the

I hold that I am a member of this body. Therefore, sir, I shall neither fawn nor cringe before any party, nor stoop to beg for my rights.

—HENRY MCNEAL TURNER, "Speech on the Eligibility of Colored Members to Seats in the Georgia Legislature," 1868 prevailing orthodoxies that they were unfit for political and social inclusion. In November 1865, hundreds of free and formerly enslaved Black men who attended the State Convention of Colored People of South Carolina signed a petition which read, in part:

> We the undersigned colored citizens of South Carolina, do respectfully ask your Honorable Body . . . that in the exercise of your high authority, over the re-establishment of civil government in South Carolina, our equal rights before the law may be respected . . . Without this political [privilege] we will have no security for our personal rights and no means to secure the blessings of education to our children.

The fifty-four-foot-long scroll that bore their signatures set forth a simple but profound demand—to be recognized before the law as full citizens. For the signatories, slavery was not a simple matter of lifting the specific legal rules that facilitated the uncompensated labor of enslaved people. The heavier lift—which was, in the end, an unsustainable one—was the challenge of dismantling a broad and deeply entrenched infrastructure that supported and sustained involuntary servitude as the presumptive status of Black people. Slavery stretched across virtually every dimension of law, including distinct private law matters pertaining to property, trusts, and estates to wider legal systems such as federalism, states' rights, constitutional jurisprudence, and the enforceability of the Bill of Rights.

It took an array of legal rules to ensure an enforceable set of practices and social conventions to sustain the perpetual bondage of more than four million people. Not only did legal rules entrap those who were formally enslaved, they also degraded the status of free Black people by enacting draconian laws grounded in the constitutionally enabled demands of enslavers. The Fugitive Slave Laws, for example, provided means for enslavers to supersede state laws to arrest and remove African Americans to the South on claims that they were runaway slaves. Such laws were Congressional efforts to ensure that the status of enslavement remained a permanent shackle for

This 54-foot-long petition bears the signatures of hundreds of men who participated in the State Convention of Colored People of South Carolina, held in Charleston, in November 1865. The petitioners asked Congress to help them secure "our equal rights before the law," including the right to vote. A number of signers, including William Beverly Nash (*above left*), later served in the state legislature during Reconstruction. Those who could not write their names signed with their marks. (See Appendix B on page 202 for transcript.)

even successfully self-liberated Black people. As a consequence of the South's successful efforts to federalize slave power, Northern states' authority to protect Black people—formerly enslaved and free—from grisly acts of violence and removal perpetrated by slave catchers was brought to heel. This Southern aggression that undermined the security of Black people in the North was far afield from the states' rights claims later made by Southern secessionists and their descendants to defend their "way of life." It was the first instance that the South effectively used federal power to trump Northern states' rights, not the other way around.

While Blackness was the "but-for" condition of enslavement—a racial status upon which enslavement was rationalized in religion, custom, and science—it was the law that gave force to the practice of equating Blackness with membership in an enslavable group. Enslavability was the ideological expression of anti-Blackness authorized and naturalized by law over time. It was a condition that resisted temporal, functional, or geographic limits. In demanding equality before the law, the freedmen correctly theorized that unequal rights reinforced their status as an enslavable people, a logic that was constitutionalized in the 1857 decision in *Dred Scott v. Sandford* denying citizenship to all people of African descent. According to Chief Justice Taney, a former slaveholder from Maryland, the status of having no rights that white men were bound to respect was the line and verse of Black enslavability. The racial burdens, legal disabilities, and societal discriminations borne by Black people everywhere in the United States were, in the end, tied together in an overarching logic that people of African descent were unfit for inclusion in the Republic and, thus, permanently excluded from the body politic.

If enslavement was rationalized by law, and if law actively facilitated the licensing of whites to inflict injury and suffering upon enslavable people, then it was well within reason for newly freed people to expect that the dismantling of enslavement would entail the repudiation of all forms of racial subordination that had enabled and enforced their previous degradation. The scope of this liberation demanded a constitutional do-over—a new foundation—that was

AMERICAN SKETCHES: A NEGRO CONGREGATION AT WASHINGTON.

based not on enslavement, but on freedom. To freed people and their Republican allies, the Reconstruction Amendments created that new foundation: The Thirteenth promised the dismantling of involuntary servitude, except for punishment; the Fourteenth provided general protections and national authority that granted citizenship at birth and promised due process and equal protection to all persons in the United States; and the Fifteenth offered political power for freedmen to protect their interests through the electoral process.

To the freed people and their most visionary allies, the Reconstruction Amendments meant that the same commitment that once underwrote the legal enforcement of slavery would now be equally effective in facilitating the institution's utter destruction. Together, these amendments were to foreground an entirely new relationship between Blackness and freedom.

A Negro Congregation at Washington, from *The Illustrated London News,* 1876. As African Americans claimed their rights as free citizens, they also claimed the right to freely practice their faith. Independent Black churches became the cornerstones of Black communities, serving as sites for schools and political meetings, as well as for religious services. After Black men gained the right to vote and run for office, many ministers also became leaders in local, state, and national politics.

And yet, the transformative objectives of the Reconstruction Amendments were never fully realized. Although law, to a far greater extent than has been recognized, was a key element in African Americans' realizing their "moment in the sun," this constitutional lodestar was utterly eclipsed by a recalcitrant Supreme Court that refused to acknowledge the profound structural transformation that the Civil War wrought. In a series of heartbreaking cases, African Americans watched as the Court, which had once located virtually limitless power to enforce slavery in the Constitution, refused to do the same to enforce freedom.

In case after case, the Supreme Court struck down or otherwise limited the newly granted powers to protect African Americans and their Republican allies from widespread discrimination and political violence. With no centralized government institution mobilized to enforce the equal rights of the freedmen—and no infrastructural protections to resist the pogroms, lynchings, and extra-legal terrorism that amplified the efforts of Southern elites to retake and redeem the South—entrenched patterns of segregation, disenfranchisement, and political repression in the waning years of Reconstruction became the norm. The rise and fall of a constitutional vision rooted in freedom still stands as the living testament to the unfinished business of Reconstruction and the role of the courts in drawing Reconstruction's many possibilities to a close.

STILL, ANOTHER PART of the unfinished business of Reconstruction is confronting and dismantling the many gendered dimensions of slavery and white supremacy. Thus, recovering Reconstruction not only entails revisiting the freedom dreams of African Americans who expected to be liberated from the burdens of enslavability, but must also recover the specific contours and reimagined trajectories of Black women's liberation. Black women's freedom dreams embraced liberation from the burdens of enslavement that they shared with their husbands, fathers, and sons, and the dimensions of their enslavability that were specifically embodied in their femaleness. They fought for Black political rights with (and sometimes against) Black men, and for suffrage with (and sometimes against) white women. They also fought for rights to be treated as ladies and mothers—rights that were denied to them as a consequence of their enslavement.

During Reconstruction, Black women confronted the subordinating myths and practices that pertained to sexuality, autonomy, and family that were historically deployed to justify their inferior status as Black women. As agents of Black freedom and producers of Black people, they too bore the weight of enslavability and of violent repression, stretching from slavery and the end of Reconstruction to present-day America. Yet the texture of their struggle and its amplification in contemporary sites of anti-Black racism are difficult to incorporate without a focused effort to recover stories that remain buried behind conventional narratives—narratives that exclude Black women from histories of racism and from histories of sexism; from histories of anti-racism and from histories of feminism.

Black women's agency tends to be erased from Reconstruction's historical record, in part because of what has been historically foregrounded as the central sites of liberation and what has been sidelined as struggles of less significance. The very fact that they were not enfranchised as former slaves means that they were both excluded from the conversation as it pertains to Black men, and treated as add-ons to white women's quest for full citizenship. Their fight for equal treatment as ladies with respect to access to public accommodations is similarly obscured within a race-only storyline about encroaching retrenchment and the Supreme Court's abandonment of freed people in the fight for freedom in public accommodations.

But there is more to be said here, both in terms of Black women's relationship to the Fifteenth Amendment and their role as shock troops in the war over the Fourteenth Amendment's utility in establishing nondiscrimination in public accommodations. As historian Elsa Barkley Brown and others have noted, Black women's political participation was vibrant through the political demands, petitions, grassroots organizing, and decision making that defined Reconstruction.

1863

Sunday, August 2.

Columbia S. C.

Reached Columbia about
six oclock Mr Whipper
met me at the depot
with his buggie, and took
me to my boarding place
where an elegant and spacious
room await to my ___ that
was tempting. My dear friend
Mr Adams came to see
me soon after my arrival
Charlotte came to see
in the morning but Kate
not. Went to Church in
morning with Harry May
and Mr Adams. the Gov
the members were there. Quite
excitement created on account
the ___appearance of Joe Har____

Because the stories of Black women are marginalized by standard record-keeping practices, the chronicle of this activism must be found in between the lines of archives and newspapers. The diary of Frances Anne Rollin Whipper, for example, is an exemplar of how the histories of political agency told by a Black woman suffragist are legible through close examination of their inner lives. Rollin was one of a set of sisters born to a free business owner in Charleston, South Carolina. Her diary detailed the daily tides, prices, and expenses of her life—events that chronicled her role as scribe for the Republican-dominated legislature. She was an influencer in Republican political circles and a fierce advocate for women's suffrage—a demand that won the support of several freedmen, but ultimately failed to muster enough support to secure proposal.

Elsewhere across the country Black women were agitating for women's suffrage, and not always in ways that simply echoed the demands of white feminists such as Susan B. Anthony and Elizabeth Cady Stanton. For example, Mary Shadd Cary, a publisher and suffragist, testified in Congress, along with several other women, presenting an argument that posited the franchise as a reparative response to enslavement. This wasn't simply an appeal for women's suffrage, but an appeal rooted in the assertion that the dismantling of slavery required not partial, but full political inclusion of formerly enslaved people. This argument contained the seeds of an alternative way of grounding women's suffrage.

The justification for the exclusion of women from the Republican vision of the expanded franchise was that the moment was "the Negro's Hour." White feminists bristled at the prioritization granted to the elimination of slavery, and notable leaders such as Anthony and Stanton devolved into racist arguments decrying the elevation of "Sambo" over the wives and sisters of white men. In their sense of righteous outrage they overlooked a potential understanding of the "Negro's Hour" that might have served as a rhetorical grounding for a gender-inclusive vision of emancipation, one in which the need to address the vulnerabilities of freedwomen, as well as freedmen, could only be addressed by empowering Black women to protect themselves as well as their families. While Black suffragists readily incorporated the eradication of conditions of servitude into their demands, among their white sisters, there seemed to be little concern for Negro women who, despite their emergence from enslavement, continued to be entrapped in the grasp of white supremacy, without agency, autonomy, or respectability.

Even conceding the historical momentum for framing the moment as the "Negro's Hour," feminists such as Anthony and Stanton could have embraced a compelling reason for supporting voting rights for Black women that might have benefitted white women's struggle for suffrage. A gender-specific addendum to the "Negro's Hour" would have placed white women as downstream *beneficiaries* of a constitutional expansion to more fully realize the emancipation of Black women. White women's failure to articulate such a radical reframing of suffrage, in the face of an uphill struggle to hitch their wagon to the Reconstructionist train, was singularly telling. Adella Hunt Logan, a Tuskegee Institute professor, summarized the need for gender-inclusive emancipation, stating, "If white American women, with all their natural and acquired advantages, need the ballot, that right protective of all other rights; if Anglo Saxons have been helped by it . . . how much more do Black Americans, male and female, need the strong defense of a vote to help secure them their right to life, liberty and the pursuit of happiness?"

Although they were denied the right to cast ballots on their own behalf, Black women were not absent bystanders in exercising political power. Black women were fierce defenders of the rights of freedmen to vote, even though support for their own rights was not fully reciprocal. Histories of Black women striving during Reconstruction attest to their efforts to shape the course of Black emancipation. Brown notes that in the early days of Reconstruction, Black women participated in community fora debating how the Black votes should be cast, and sometimes provided armed protection to ensure that Black men could cast their ballots. Their mobilization, agitation, advocacy, and agenda-setting may escape the official record of Black legislative initiatives, but descriptions of their participation in church and organization meetings evidence extraordinary activism. Black women's political agency was also marked by those who resorted to racial terror to complete disenfranchisement: Ben "Pitchfork" Tillman, a murderous politician who galvanized white supremacist desires into brutal pogroms to extinguish political participation by freed people, preached that Black women could never be enfranchised given their recalcitrance in the face of oppression.

The history of Black women's political agency during Reconstruction has yet to be fully told, but their dynamism continues to resonate through contemporary community activists, mobilizers, and scribes—all of which are vitally important roles in transforming individual voting rights into group power. During Reconstruction, these roles existed whether or not Black women could individually exercise their right to vote.

ASIDE FROM POLITICAL AGITATION and participation, Black women sought their freedom dreams in ways that marked the gendered particulars of enslavement. Their ways of enacting their own sense of liberation underscore how slavery constructed concepts of family, gender, autonomy, and sexual agency. In pushing against slavery's conventions during Reconstruction, formerly enslaved women took on and repudiated gendered dimensions of the all-encompassing dimensions of the institution. Although their actions risk displacement by the detailed histories of Black men and white women fighting against racialized and gendered marginality, Black women's refusals to abide by the logics of their supposed lesser womanhood mark the unique ways that they struggled to realize the implications of emancipation.

For Black women, a system of industrialized rape-for-profit and subsequent alienation from their children underwrote slavery's enormous profitability. Both sexual coercion and the utterly inhumane alienation of their children were practices that were buttressed, facilitated, and insulated by law. More broadly, the ideological construction of Black women as female livestock framed them as a species inherently distinct from white women—a framing that left them outside of the concomitants of womanhood. Defined as essentially "unrapable," the rape of female slaves was generally not regarded as a crime—a lack of protection that extended beyond the formalities of enslavement to free Black women during and after slavery.

In tandem with the legal facilitation of rape was the denial of Black women's ability to defend themselves from unwanted sexual encounters. The 1855 execution of nineteen-year-old Celia, an enslaved woman, revealed the legal consequences of Black women's assertion of self-defense. Celia was convicted of "felonious and willful murder" for physically defending herself from the man who had repeatedly raped and brutalized her since she was fourteen. Her subsequent execution for killing her rapist—who was also her owner—evidences how Black women were systematically excluded from the rights that women were thought to exercise even in a sexist system. This embodiment of sexual racism rooted in slavery is often obscured by the fact that even a rumor of a Black man looking at a white woman "the wrong way" underwrote the brutalization and murders of Black men. Yet, while the brutal consequences of breaching the zone of protection around white women was a universally recognized embodiment of white supremacy, the fact that repeated physical assault could not justify a Black woman's attempt to protect herself has been far less salient as a site of racist power.

Black women during Reconstruction and its aftermath understood that their degraded status as women was a critical site from which to declare their freedom. Diaries of white mistresses and records of Union officers reveal how freedwomen directly and immediately contested the gendered norms of slavery that had long denied Black women the rights of womanhood, motherhood, and ladyhood. Resentful mistresses wrote of how newly freed women presented themselves as ladies and homemakers, leaving behind the fantasy of the trusted and loyal slave to their mistresses who resented their departure and their self-representation as ladies. Letters by plantation mistresses reflected their shock and dismay in response to the self-liberation of formerly enslaved women who "abandoned" them in pursuit of their own liberation. Their protests—often dripping with a sense of hurt, betrayal, and vengeance—reveal how Black women's freedom disrupted their former mistresses' expectations of loyalty and obedience, fantasies predicated on their own denial about the nature of relationships grounded in unyielding coercion.

Black women understood that servitude was not merely an arrangement of labor, but a platform upon which the superiority of whiteness was grounded and performed in countless ways, including dress and comportment. Writing about freedwomen eschewing the confining white expectations of their degraded womanhood, Thavolia Glymph notes, "in parading as ladies, Black women struck a deliberately targeted blow at racism and the pedestal of Southern white womanhood. These parades, loud and boisterous as parades tend to be, actually began before the war, but it was only in the context of the war and the slaves' emancipation that they came to be viewed by more than a minority of white Southerners as subversive. With freedom's arrival, the parades became evermore ostentatious, amazing public spectacles acted out."

As Reconstruction progressed, freedwomen's fight to be afforded the dignity of proper treatment as ladies was sometimes victorious and sometimes defeated. Still, the struggle can be found in the numerous records of their protests in public spaces, particularly as middle-class Black women became mobile and demanded access to the ladies' car. Frances Anne Rollin Whipper, Ida B. Wells, Mary Church Terrell, Frances Ellen Watkins Harper, and others chronicled how the developing practice of race segregation was largely a story of Black women and their escorts gaining access to the ladies' car and then subsequently losing their right to ride in safety and comfort. For Black women leaders coming of age during the denouement of Reconstruction, the experience of being thrown off of trains, humiliated, and embarrassed was almost a rite of passage, passed on like a baton from Harriet Tubman and Sojourner Truth, towering figures who, years earlier, encountered physical abuse in

Portrait of a woman, ca. mid-1800s. During the Reconstruction era, Black women took varied and concerted actions to claim their freedom, define their political and social status, and assert their womanhood. An act as seemingly simple as sitting for a photograph provided an empowering opportunity for a Black woman to break free of the confining, distorting lens of white society and present herself to the world as she desired to be seen.

resisting denigrating treatment in public accommodations.

In the early years of Reconstruction, some Black women sought protection against discrimination by filing lawsuits. Frances Anne Rollin Whipper became one of the first women whose suit against the conductor of a steamboat for his refusal to permit her to occupy first-class accommodations was recorded. There, a military court ruled in her favor and rewarded her monetary damages. This struggle for respectable service continued throughout Reconstruction to its conclusion, with Black women sometimes victorious in their initial complaints, only to be overturned as the hardening race lines reversed the fleeting progress that Black women made in seeking equalization with white women.

We must keep on talking, protesting, praying, appealing, and agitating—but we must do more—we must ACT and ACT NOW, PROMPTLY AND VIGOROUSLY. The way is clear. We have health, we have strength, we have intelligence, we have money—let us use all of these God-given elements to win our battle for liberty, opportunity, and social justice.

—IDA B. WELLS, speech at Asbury Methodist Episcopal Church in Washington, DC, 1917

Typical of this contestation was a lawsuit brought in 1883 by Ida B. Wells. Traveling between Memphis and her place of employment, she had initially been seated in a car primarily filled with men, sometimes called the smoking car because it was there that men were permitted to smoke, chew tobacco, and engage in other raucous behavior free from the expectations of gentility to which ladies were entitled. Wells moved to the ladies' car and was instructed to leave because of her race. When she refused to relinquish her seat, she was forcibly expelled from the train as both white men and women applauded. Wells sued the railroad on the grounds that she was illegally denied the right to occupy the ladies' car. She initially won her lawsuit, but thereafter lost on appeal at the Tennessee Supreme Court.

Sallie Robinson also challenged her expulsion from the ladies' car, arguing that the conductor's refusal to permit her and her young nephew to occupy the ladies' car was race discrimination prohibited by the Civil Rights Act of 1875. The railroad denied her claim, arguing that the indignity was not due to a categorical assumption that Black women did not warrant inclusion in the ladies' car, but due instead to the mistaken assumption that she, as a Black woman traveling with a young man who appeared to be white, was a woman of ill-repute. The racist dimensions of "ill-repute," which bore heavily upon Black women, were fully apparent in the facts of the case—one of several cases that would subsequently yield a devastating blow in the landmark Supreme Court opinion in 1883 overturning the Civil Rights Act of 1875.

In an opinion that effectively ended the decades-long campaign of numerous Black women to secure access to accommodations that were readily available to similarly situated white women, the Supreme Court fully submerged the particulars of Robinson's claim in a fiction that no federal intervention was warranted or constitutionally authorized. This claim was based on a

The Chesapeake, Ohio and Southwestern Railroad v. Ida Wells, 1885. After a white conductor forced Ida B. Wells off a train for refusing to move out of the first-class car, Wells sued the railroad company for damages. The Circuit Court of Shelby County ruled in Wells's favor, stating that she was "refused the first-class accommodations to which she was entitled under the law." The Supreme Court of Tennessee overturned the decision on appeal.

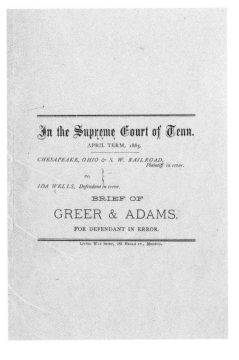

position that freedmen stood equal before the state laws and should thus resort to ordinary means to enforce their rights. Justice Bradley's admonishment to Black men to cease being "the special favourites of the law" completely sidestepped the special treatment that lay at the heart of ladies' car discrimination against Black women. This rigid distinction between the most-favored status afforded to white women was simultaneously denied to freedwomen. Racial hierarchy between women was, thus, a foundational dimension of the hardening of the racial divide—a reflection of a battle fought and, for a time, lost by Black women. And it was a battle that they could not win support from their supposed allies in the suffrage movement.

As the deteriorating status of Black women in public space continued during Reconstruction's overthrow, they appealed to leaders of the suffragist movement to denounce the ill-treatment they endured when traveling by train to attend suffragist conventions. Susan B. Anthony refused, making it clear that suffrage—not race discrimination—was the *exclusive* concern of the feminist movement of the time.

At the core of the contestation over Black women's respectability is and has always been the ever-present legacy of slavery's institutionalized sexual violence. While there is some evidence that Black women found a sympathetic ear among the military governments during the war—and presumably greater access to formal charges once the barriers to giving testimony against white men were lifted—a missing dimension of Reconstruction's story is the extent to which Black women sought greater protections against the sexual abuse that was so central to slavery.

As lynching and other forms of sexual racism took center stage in the justifications of racist violence, the realities of Black women's vulnerability were sidelined not only by the purveyors of the mythical Black rapist, but also by those who sought to reveal the political and economic agendas that drove lynching and other acts of racial terror. The myriad ways that Black women were subjugated through sexual racism remained significantly less visible as a specific site of anti-Black racism and resistance to it.

MISS GARRITY.
PHOTOGRAPHER.   CHICAGO.

Portrait of Ida B. Wells, ca. 1893. Born in Mississippi in 1862, Wells attended college and worked as a schoolteacher before rising to prominence as a journalist and civil rights activist. Her campaign against lynching brought worldwide attention to racial violence and injustice in the Jim Crow South.

Recovering this site of power and resistance uncovers the largely unappreciated dynamic in which Black women were silently signified in the white male preoccupation with the safety of white women. The historian Crystal Feimster reveals how the trope of Black male rapists functionally projects the history of white male sexual aggression against Black women onto the supposed vulnerability of white women to Black male aggression. Feimster writes,

"Whereas prior to the war, abolitionists had espoused a political narrative that centered on the rape of Black women by white men, in the post-war years Southern white men developed a political discourse that defined a rape as a crime committed by Black men against white women. In constructing the image of the 'Black rapist,' Southern white men sought to challenge Black men's and women's rights as Citizens, while expanding their own sexual power over African Americans." The twisted logic by which Black women's vulnerability to white sexual aggression was erased and replaced by the myth of white women's vulnerability to Black men conveys a fuller story of the racial oppression that Black women sought to be liberated from during Reconstruction.

Almost a century and a half after Reconstruction's end, Susie Jackson's life was extinguished by a child possessed by the Black sexual aggression fantasy that emerged as a tool of white heteropatriarchy. His robotic repetition of the age-old myth that "[Black people] are raping our women and taking over the world" is as destructive as racism's underrecognized lethality against Black women.

If Black women's particularly gendered vulnerability to white supremacy was more fully grasped, then the unspeakable tragedy of Susie Jackson—a Black woman who lived for nearly a century was much more likely to be raped than to give birth to the Bigger Thomas of the hysterically racist mind—would be mourned as an embodiment of Reconstruction's arrested promise to Black women.

The historic flattening of Black women's protest and agency is ever present. This misremembering, this failure to fully engage these histories, has had consequences. Recovering these freedom dreams demands revisiting the moments of struggle equipped with the capacity to elevate the multiple ways that white supremacy was engendered as well as the legacies of Black women who struggled to resist it.

IN THE AFTERMATH of Bree Newsome's momentous climb, many of those closest to her warned that her story might well be told the same way that Rosa Parks's was. Newsome recalls that some observers of Black women's political history warned: "Don't let them Rosa Parks you. Don't allow people to turn you into some kind of symbol that they can use for their own agenda and tell you to just be quiet. That's really what they meant, and that's what I came to recognize."

Indeed, Rosa Parks's famous and meticulously planned protest—the one that launched the Montgomery bus boycotts of 1955—is often summarized in history books as the result of her "being tired." Unknown to too many, Parks didn't stumble into history because her feet were sore. In fact, she had been fighting for intersectional justice for Black women for years. Parks herself said, "The only tired I was, was tired of giving in." A seasoned organizer and activist, Parks, like Newsome generations later, was not acting on impulse. Her action was grounded in years of organizing experience.

News photograph of Recy Taylor, 1944. After six white men abducted and raped her one night on her way home from church in Abbeville, Alabama, Taylor refused to remain silent. She reported the crime to authorities, and when they refused to charge her attackers, she told her story to the press. Taylor's determination to seek justice, despite threats to her life and family, exposed the assaults on freedom, security, and dignity that Black women confronted in their daily lives.

And yet even when her activism in the bus boycotts is accurately portrayed, we hear little about her as a women's rights advocate. We do not hear that in 1944, a young Parks led a national campaign for justice on behalf of another Black woman, Recy Taylor. We learn little about Taylor, a twenty-four-year-old wife and mother from Abbeville, Alabama, who was raped by six white men on her way home from church on September 3, 1944. Through Parks's involvement, the NAACP arranged for coverage of Taylor's case in the *Chicago Defender* and her story made national headlines. Letter-writing campaigns and political pressure forced the local prosecutor to empanel a grand jury—a colossal feat led by Parks.

Six decades after emancipation, Taylor's rapists claimed that their assault was actually consensual sex work and her husband was offered $600 in exchange for his silence. The grand jury ultimately refused to issue an indictment. Its refusal was deeply grounded in the sexual myths produced by the ideology of Black women's enslavability, stretching from the period of formal enslavement to mid-twentieth-century America.

The realities of Black women's resistance to sexual abuse, rooted in enslavement, is a dimension of freedom dreaming that was amplified during Reconstruction and extends to this day. Yet these dreams are not formally catalogued in the historical record as liberationist actions. As a consequence, Black women's contemporary activations against sexual abuse and sexual harassment have too often been disregarded as white women's issues. Such historically inaccurate claims were made when Anita Hill offered testimony in 1992 that she had been harassed by then-Supreme Court nominee Clarence Thomas. The "misremembering" of Black women's vulnerability and political agency has not only marginalized Black women in the historical record of Reconstruction and beyond, it has also truncated the availability of the long arc of Black freedom struggle as a platform for contemporary action.

One can only dream about how sexual harassment and assault would be centered as a form of anti-Black racism if Rosa Parks's entry into the American imagination began when she was a rape-crisis advocate for Recy Taylor. In curating the memory of Black freedom struggles, we must ask, "What if Rosa Parks could be liberated from her gilded seat on that Montgomery bus?" From there, we can envision a different world—politically, constitutionally, and socially—if race and gender had not been violently torn apart when Anita Hill came forward to tell her story.

Recovering lost freedom dreams from Reconstruction helps us think about how different movements, practices, and workplaces would look today if the past was told to us more fully—not broken into pieces along lines of race *and* gender. What would it mean for the descendants of slaves, and for Black women more specifically, to uncover examples of their leadership and agendas that were forgotten because the authors of Reconstruction never fought to fully liberate freedwomen from slavery's scourge along with freedmen? What would it mean to interrogate and upend, once and for all, the myth of enslavability through a fully intersectional lens—one that attends to the ways that the aftermath of enslavement shaped the lives of slavery's descendants across gender?

Looking to Reconstruction is a reminder that spectacular acts of resistance like Bree Newsome's climb or Rosa Parks's stance on the bus were not isolated incidents; they were not historical accidents in which the subjects of Black resistance were only episodically women. Although these moments capture the public imagination (Black and white alike), although they are embraced by the media and sometimes praised by political leaders, and although they are written about over and over again, these incidents are simply the tip of a long-submerged iceberg. If we look past the immediate spectacle of these moments, we see long histories and wide networks of Black women working behind the scenes: activists leading community organizations; orators inspiring everyday people; organizers offering aid and assistance door-to-door; volunteers filing paperwork to keep the lights on at headquarters. These everyday actions do not get featured in documentaries of past struggles, celebrated in the heroic narratives of the movement's great leaders, or rehearsed in primetime Black History Month specials. But these everyday actions of everyday Black women have been the beating heart of the Black freedom struggle from Reconstruction onward. And if stories of Black women's defiance in the face of their marginality are recovered, then historical memory and its artifacts could get us closer to a moment where the image of a Black woman taking down the flag is not so unsettling and unrecognizable. If we excavate the true legacies of Black women's resistance undergirding our historic struggle for freedom, we can build a more robust vision of liberation.

This pursuit of liberation is echoed in the #SayHerName Campaign, an effort to draw attention to the ways that anti-Black police violence is gendered. In 2014, the African American Policy Forum launched the #SayHerName Campaign to elevate the often-invisible stories of Black women and girls killed by the police and other agents of the state. Bearing witness to the lives and stories of Black women like Eleanor Bumpurs, Ayanna Stanley Jones, Kayla Moore, Michelle Cusseaux, India Kager, Korryn Gaines, Tanisha Anderson, and so many more revealed how that lack of a narrative frame, linking the past to the present, allows the stolen lives of Black women to slip from our societal consciousness. In tandem with these erasures is the unreckoned sexual abuse of Black women by police, as amplified by the little-reported conviction of Daniel Holtzclaw for the rape of multiple Black women. Police violence that is sexual, and sexual violence by state actors, falls far outside the historical frames that have been rehearsed over time to address police abuse and gender-based violence. As a consequence of Black women's marginality as subjects of both, reporters don't tell their stories, communities don't organize around them, and policy makers don't address the causes or the effects of the violence perpetrated against them. Sandra Bland and Breonna Taylor are exceptions to the invisibility that bestows to mourning families their loss.

The imperative to #SayHerName echoes across the generations as a reminder to revisit the histories of struggle and liberation that are not included in the conventional telling of our history. When our rich history must be recovered from layers of untold narratives, cemented by myths about Reconstruction's failures, and naturalized by uncontested beliefs grounded in white supremacy, the opportunity to deepen the recovery must not go unheeded. By taking the time to speak the names, stories, and work of Black women from Reconstruction to today, we reanimate their freedom dreams and recolor a fuller vision for Black liberation. These vivid illustrations might finally chart our path toward the double recovery of race and gender from the grips of a past unconfronted.

• • •

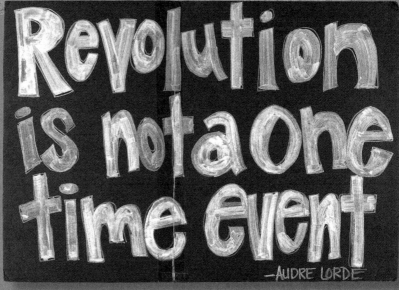

Above: #SayHerName campaign activists at the Women's March on Washington, January 21, 2017. The march provided a venue for hundreds of thousands to protest and give voice on the National Mall and across the nation to deep-rooted connections between issues of gender, sexuality, race, oppression, and liberation. A protester's poster from the march (*bottom*) quotes self-described "Black lesbian, mother, warrior, poet" Audre Lorde: "Revolution is not a one-time event."

LEGACIES
OF
VIOLENCE

Kidada E. Williams

Scenes in Memphis, Tennessee, During the Riot—Shooting Down Negroes on the Morning of May 2, 1866 (detail). From *Harper's Weekly.* Less than a month after Congress passed the Civil Rights Act of 1866, which defined African Americans as equal citizens under the law, the city of Memphis erupted in three days of violent racial backlash. The Memphis massacre presaged a pattern of white attacks on Black freedom that aimed to undermine and negate the political gains of Reconstruction.

TODAY'S DEATHS AND INJURIES from state and racist vigilante violence are part of a descending line of state and vigilante violence dating back to Reconstruction. United in grief and grievance, African Americans and their allies know this history, which is why, amid a global pandemic, George Floyd's murder by a Minneapolis police officer set off collective outrage and protests around the world.

Floyd's brother, Mr. Philonise Floyd, in his testimony during a US House of Representatives Judiciary Committee oversight hearing on policing and law enforcement accountability, referring to police officers' use of excessive force, asked the Congress and the nation to "make it stop." He also remarked, "I couldn't take care of George that day he was killed, but maybe by speaking with you today, I can make sure that his death will not be in vain. To make sure that he is more than another face on a tee shirt, more than another name on a list that won't stop growing."

Philonise Floyd attends a Congressional hearing on June 10, 2020, to testify about the killing of his brother, George Floyd, by Minneapolis police. Philonise's mask bears a picture of his brother and the words "I can't breathe," which were spoken by George as a police officer crushed his neck. In his testimony, Philonise urged lawmakers to hold police accountable. "George called for help and he was ignored," he said. "Please listen to the call I'm making to you now."

In recent years, Americans have learned of the police killings of unarmed Black people and have observed law enforcement lie, bury police malfeasance, exonerate officers, and blame victims for their own murders. Many non-Black Americans accept law enforcement's version, which enables law enforcement and the nation to move on. But for the victims' kin, like Mr. Floyd, and for Black Americans who experience and live under the threat of state or vigilante violence, these killings and the state's use of the law as a shield against truth are an injustice, which gave rise to the Movement for Black Lives and #SayHerName, a campaign protesting police violence against Black girls and women.

Mr. Floyd testified because he understood that each time Americans allow law enforcement to commit murder, ignore officers' violations of their duty to protect and serve, and to decline to prosecute police who have killed unarmed people, they lay the groundwork for more killings. This helix of murder, its acceptance, and Black people's resistance to it are rooted in Reconstruction, a time of reprisal attacks on African Americans.

Americans are inundated by an inaccurate white supremacist history of the Reconstruction era, which states that peace at the end of the Civil War was achieved by diplomatic, formal electoral politics between North and South, Democrats and Republicans, the federal government, and the states. In this white-washed version, the Civil War was a conflict involving "brother against brother," divided by secession. Reunifying the nation was a slow, but largely positive political endeavor among the white brothers, marred only by freeing African Americans and giving them the franchise. Former Confederates redeemed their honor and preserved white supremacy by forming the Ku Klux Klan, and peace was achieved.

Such a tale seems easy—too easy—because civil wars never end this neatly. Americans have created so many falsehoods about Reconstruction that it is hard to blame them for not recognizing the truth, i.e., the idea of Black people enjoying American freedom so offended white nationalists they overthrew Reconstruction by waging war on them and it.

THE HISTORY OF THE CIVIL WAR era shows that Black people, by taking their collective destiny into their own hands, through escaping bondage or fighting slavery where they were held, waged war against slavery as fiercely as Confederates waged the war in favor of the "peculiar institution." By tapping into that spirit, with victory on the Civil War battlefields at hand, Black freedom fighters campaigned for legal freedom, pushing lawmakers to pass the Thirteenth Amendment, and then insisted on the right to secure it by demanding formally recognized rights to be active participants in American life.

The prospect of making freedom real was not something that African Americans like Warren Jones, who lived through emancipation, took lightly. The historian Ira Berlin referred to these newly manumitted people as the "Freedom Generation." For them, freedom revolved around family restoration and protection.

Thirty-five-year-old Jones, of Warren County, Georgia, was eager to build a future with his wife and son. Jones likely envisioned home and landownership in his future. He probably intended to send his son to the school being established in his community and to pass on his work ethic and the fruits of his labor. For Jones's dreams of freedom for his family to become a reality, he needed fair employment, land, and property. Men like Jones wanted voting rights and the eligibility to run for public office, in service of their people, because law and policy were needed to protect families from discriminatory legislation such as the Black codes. These were restrictive laws that former slaveholding states established to limit Black people's progress by denying them freedom of movement and criminalizing circumstances such as Black unemployment.

This is why African Americans insisted that lawmakers turn the many liberties and freedoms whites took for granted into legally protected *rights* that all Americans enjoyed. These liberties included the ability to vote, marry, and practice one's religion. The freedoms encompassed the legitimate authority to receive an education, as well as to move about as one pleased.

Vested with certain civil rights and recognition as the head of household denied him during slavery, Jones negotiated a contract with a white cotton-producing landowner named Obadiah Laseter. Laseter would provide land and horses, and Jones would work the land for half the crop yield, some horse feed, and would also pay for blacksmithing. His contract with Laseter was the first leg of his freedom journey.

During the growing season, Jones worked hard and was industrious enough to hire someone to increase his yield, which produced thirty bags of cotton. When he approached Laseter for his share, he refused and told him to keep working.

Understanding the reality of his financial insecurity with Laseter made Jones eager to strike out for opportunities elsewhere. Laseter told Jones that if he tried to leave, he would set the Klan on him. As evidence of African Americans' capacity to transcend slavery bore fruit, whites, like Obadiah Laseter, were determined to have a servile domestic and agricultural labor force. With the nearest troops 120 miles away in Atlanta, there was no one to stop men like him from halting African Americans' ascent.

Jones knew what would happen if white men came for him. At the least, he and his people would be brutalized. At the worst, they could be killed. Jones's appreciation of his family's vulnerability was underscored when neighbors warned him that Laseter boasted about killing him if he tried to leave. Jones tried to delay his departure by joining other targeted people sleeping away from their homes at night. When a gang came into his yard, Jones and everyone else knew they were there for him, so he made a break for it. Jones was lucky. He and his family slipped away without being detected. Thousands of other families were not as fortunate.

In 1867–68, African Americans' participation in the first elections kicked the war on freedom into high gear. Conservatives formed paramilitary groups and started a reign of terror. The Ku Klux Klan became the most popular, but most white vigilantes were not members of groups.

The Klan Hearings occurred in 1871. Warren Jones was one of the witnesses who testified in Atlanta. With the prospect of the prosecution of the guilty parties untenable, federal officials chose alternative legal and legislative responses, including establishing the Joint Committee to Inquire into the Conditions of Affairs in the Late Insurrectionary States. The hearings had a razor-thin scope—they were seeking information about civic disenfranchisement, not justice.

Jones had been among the thousands whose freedom was undone by being forced to choose between their families' lives and their rights. In making that choice, Jones and his family had to live with the repercussions, chased by white supremacy's vengeful flame. Like many African Americans displaced by white terror, Jones explained his troubles when he moved his family to Atlanta, saying, "When I came here, I did not have a cent in the world." For the thirty bags of cotton he picked, which averaged 501 pounds each, Jones and his people should have received fourteen cents a pound. At the end of the season, there were 15,030 pounds of

Proceedings of the Ku Klux Trials. The Enforcement Acts, passed by Congress in 1870 and 1871, empowered the federal government to prosecute the Ku Klux Klan and others who conspired to prevent Black men from voting. During federal grand jury investigations, hundreds of African Americans came forward to testify about being terrorized by the Klan. In South Carolina, this testimony led to the indictment of 220 Klansmen for civil rights violations, but only five were ultimately tried and convicted.

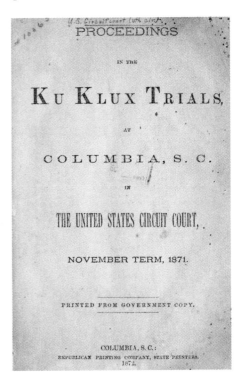

THE MASKED SENTINEL.

The Masked Sentinel, 1879. This illustration appeared in *A Fool's Errand*, an account of the Ku Klux Klan's terrorist activities written by white attorney and civil rights activist Albion Tourgée. The uniform white robes and pointed hoods associated with the modern Ku Klux Klan did not appear until the 1900s. During the organization's first phase in the 1860s and 1870s, Klan members wore various disguises while terrorizing local citizens—many of whom knew and recognized the men despite their masks.

cotton worth $2,104.20. Jones said Laseter owed him $1,052, the equivalent of thousands more today. Moving to Atlanta burned through Jones's financial reserves. His new earnings were nothing close to what he lost.

"The Ku-Klux were very thick," Jones said. He had seen and heard of squads of armed white men mobilizing and attacking Blacks and telling them they couldn't find independent work without permission from their current employer. The men wore costumes, used false names, and claimed they were ghosts from the 1863 battle at Manassas Gap. African Americans knew they were not ghosts.

Jones surmised that whites "supposed the negroes would get together to talk politics," which would further Black independence, so white vigilante groups whipped Black people, denied them the right to assemble, and burned down their meeting places. Within three weeks of its opening, whites destroyed a school that African Americans in Jones's community had financed. The vigilantes targeted churches, killing ministers and burning houses of worship. They killed Black landowners and entrepreneurs, and rallied to crush people resisting oppressive work conditions. White terror gangs claimed that without slavery, Black men were out of control and attacking white people.

Jones said, "they have no law down there except what they make themselves, for colored men to go by." White Southerners' refusal to accept the new legal order and authorities' failure to enforce the new legislation and amendments affirmed Jones's conclusion.

Rather than see the First Reconstruction Act's civic enfranchisement of Black men as aligning the nation's deeds with its founding documents, white Georgians like Laseter thought their standing in society would diminish if African Americans gained equal access

There has been much opposition to the School. Twice I have been shot at in my room. Some of my night school scholars have been shot but none killed. . . . The rebels here threatened to burn down the school and house in which I board . . . But I trust fearlessly in God and am safe.

—EDMONIA G. HIGHGATE, teacher's letter to secretary of the American Missionary Association, 1866 to economic and political power. Whites who did not support Black self-determination lashed out at Black people. White employers threatened Black workers who insisted on being paid for their labor and their right to come and go without white people's permission. White voters and politicians attacked elected officials and threatened Blacks who voted for progressive candidates. This was not enough to stop the Freedom Generation, however. They organized into independent, armed Black militias to advance and protect their political and economic goals for voting, serving in office, and acquiring land. White supremacists exacted revenge. By 1868, roving mobs of heavily armed white men began terrorizing communities by day and at night. Mustering and disbanding quickly, just before elections or before newly elected officials took office, they launched campaigns against Black politicians, voters, and officeholders.

Planters near Aberdeen, Mississippi, ordered their Black laborers to vote the conservative Democrat ticket and threatened to have the Klan attack them if they did not comply. On election day, armed white men were at the polls and refused to give Black men their ballots, stealing the election. Afterward, they menaced the Black men's families and attacked those who protested this mistreatment. When John Childers, a forty-two-year-old, Sumter County, Alabama resident cursed white men attacking Blacks in his community, a white man heard and confronted him. When Childers defended his right to protest unprovoked attacks, three white men retaliated, beating him over the head with double-barreled shotguns. Childers also testified at the Klan Hearings. He said, "They beat me, and knocked me, and did everything a man could do to a man except kill him. They didn't quite kill me." Bands like Childers's assailants often formed spontaneously, making it difficult to defend against their assaults, and for local and state authorities that respected Black people's rights to address.

People targeted by white supremacist violence informed local magistrates and Freedmen's Bureau agents, but federal and state officials lacked the will to restrain the violence. This indifference inspired white riots and massacres, the most noted of which were

From the 1870s to the 1890s, groups of armed white men wearing red shirts like this one terrorized and murdered Black voters in Southern states. The Red Shirts served as a para-military arm of the Democratic Party, using violence and intimidation to overthrow the Republican-led Reconstruction state governments and restore white supremacist rule in the South. Their campaign of terror succeeded. In the picture (*above*), Red Shirts gather to intimidate voters at a polling place in North Carolina.

in Memphis and New Orleans, in 1866, and Colfax, Louisiana, in 1873. In Memphis and New Orleans, white mobs and gangs, which included policemen, elected officials, and businessmen, instigated the violence and targeted African Americans and destroyed most of their homes, schools, churches, and businesses. When Black people defended themselves, whites slaughtered them. In Memphis, forty-six Black people, most of whom were Union veterans, were killed and dozens wounded; five were raped. In New Orleans, approximately fifty Black people were killed and nearly 150 were wounded. In Colfax, a Black militia, afraid that white people would violently seize control of their parish's governance occupied the local courthouse. A white mob fired a cannon inside sparking an initial shootout. When the outnumbered Black men surrendered, the mob massacred them.

White violence accomplished what its agents intended—it disenfranchised Black voters, drove Black lawmakers from office, stripped Black people of their land, and left their bodies and minds with life-altering injuries, enabling former Confederates to regain control of local and state offices. They bulldozed Reconstruction policies, but African Americans refused to surrender their claims to them, so the violence continued.

Some Southern, white, progressive governors declared martial law or requested federal troops. Congress passed the Enforcement Acts, which outlawed the use of masks and disguises and made it a federal offense to interfere with voting and serving in office. President Ulysses S. Grant sent troops to certain areas to reduce violence, and federal agents to investigate and arrest perpetrators, but where the troops advanced, the terror gangs retreated only to emerge in other communities. Black men in places such as Hamburg, South Carolina, and Grant Parish, Louisiana, formed militias to try to beat back some attackers, but they were often outgunned and outmanned.

Federal officials tried prosecuting white terror gangs, but even functioning legal systems struggle to handle the magnitude of genocidal violence. The war against freedom pit the former slaveholding states against the federal government, which continued to assert new, highly contested powers that allowed Congress and the president to enforce the Reconstruction Amendments' protections of African Americans' rights, and to send troops to end the disorder. With Southern whites serving on federal juries and opposing the federal government's right to even conduct the trials of Klansmen, few terrorists prosecuted in South Carolina were convicted or served time.

Meanwhile, whites in Northern and Western states were growing impatient with the nation's fixation on administering freedom and democracy in the former slaveholding states. Like most societies following atrocities, those who weren't targeted, or those who benefited, simply wanted to move on.

In inviting Black survivors to participate in the Klan Hearings, the Congress of 1871, like the Congress of 2020's Oversight Hearing on Policing Practices and Law Enforcement Accountability, allowed victims to enter their stories into the historical record and, like Philonise Floyd, the Freedom Generation wanted the nation to bring to a stop the violent infringement on the rights of Black people. The injustice of losing their kin, rights, and homes, and the hope for ending the violence steeled families to go forward and communicate the evil done to them and demand justice. They bared their souls and displayed their injuries detailing the many facets of their harrowing experiences.

John Childers explained the politically motivated attacks on him, but broke protocol at the Livingston, Alabama, hearings by sharing the story of his daughter, Amanda's, killing. Childers saw her death as part of the war on freedom, even if lawmakers did not. He knew lawmakers only wanted to hear stories of election violence, but Amanda mattered, and he believed that the killing needed an accounting.

While Childers was traveling and managing his family's affairs, his wife, Julia, arranged for their daughter, Amanda, to work for a white family. When he returned on June 30, 1870, he observed the girl behaving oddly, and asked her about it. She replied, "Mr. Jones beat me nearly to death." Childers saw that she had been "awfully badly whipped," and there were great gashes on her thighs, "as long as my finger," he said.

The family treated Amanda's wounds and tried to keep her comfortable. Soon, she "started sweating a lot," as her body tried to fight off an infection. They called a doctor who diagnosed her with "congestion of the brains." Amanda died just before her tenth birthday. The authorities charged the man who beat her, and the men who assaulted Childers, but their allies ran witnesses off, Childers said, as he wept at the injustice.

African American survivors of white terrorist attacks, like Warren Jones and John Childers, may not have had a name for the force that cast their families into the whirlwind of white supremacist hate that prevented them from being truly free. But their testimonies make it clear that these brave men wanted the nation to know that the deaths and the losses of livelihoods they suffered were grievable. They called upon the nation to honor the promise of freedom and equal protection. However, the nation failed, abandoning the law and any promise of democracy. Jones and Childers knew the wickedness of the violence done to them. They were revictimized by the cruelty of the nation's betrayal.

Aided by white, conservative lawmakers who asked questions that sought to discredit survivors, white terrorists like Laseter lied and assailed African Americans' testimonies about the destruction of their lives and dignity. White supremacist media justified the deaths and papered over the injustices. In suppressing and discrediting survivors' accounts, whites started erasing the horrors of the genocidal violence that they used to regain political power.

Ex-Confederates dismantled many of the last vestiges of Reconstruction, then they manufactured an apocryphal tale, twisting the history of the Civil War era. They erased African Americans from the history of the war, especially their flights from slavery and into military service. When they included Black people, they portrayed them as undeserving of freedom and democracy.

White supremacists claimed that Black people were incapable of self-governance, which is why they drove Black men from the polls and out of office. The supremacists did not mention the acts they committed, including assassinations and holding families hostage in their homes, while subjecting them to torture. White supremacists said Black people struggled to earn a living because they did not have the same work ethic, but did not mention white people's theft of money and land. By concluding that Black people failed to live up to the potential of freedom, white Americans absolved themselves, in the name of the reunification of the nation, compounding the injustice survivors experienced. The lack of meaningful punishment and white Americans' embrace of a false narrative wiped the slate clean. Victims of future racist violence would be met with a lie perfected at this time—no violence happened. If any did, no one was responsible, and anyone who was cannot be held accountable. Election violence continued and went unchecked with no formal accounting for African Americans' deaths and ongoing suffering. With each brick stacked and bed of mortar spread on what was becoming the fortress of the Lost Cause narrative of Reconstruction, an exonerating tale of the white peace overrode all others shaping American memory and perception.

Nonetheless, African Americans who seized freedom challenged the white history of Reconstruction for as long as they could. Because their injuries were ongoing and being inflicted anew, for targeted people, attacks were never in the past. In bearing witness to the destruction of freedom, they created the archive of Reconstruction's overthrow, challenging the Lost Cause mythology.

Future historians wrote accurate accounts of Reconstruction. W.E.B. Du Bois knew whites used the twisted history of Reconstruction to justify disenfranchisement, economic exploitation, and segregation. So when whites responded to Black people's resistance by resorting to the terrorism perfected during Reconstruction, he connected older atrocities to contemporary ones. In *Black Reconstruction*, Du Bois detailed Black people's role in expanding American freedom and the price they paid. White supremacists sustained their fictions but future historians substantiated his claims.

Du Bois lived through mass-killing events where thousands of whites spurred by lies or a belief in their right to rule, replicated the earlier rampages by roaming the streets, slaughtering African

The white supremacist terror campaigns that began during Reconstruction reached a horrific climax on November 10, 1898, in Wilmington, North Carolina. Declaring war on "Negro domination," armed mobs of Red Shirts and militia men attacked Black neighborhoods and overthrew the city government, which was led by an interracial board of aldermen. Black leaders were arrested and forced out of town. Here, the mob stands in front of the destroyed offices of the *Daily Record*, Wilmington's Black newspaper.

Americans and destroying their cherished institutions and businesses. He noted the 1898 massacre and coup in Wilmington, North Carolina, where Black people had made great strides and white supremacists upended everything they had accomplished.

Du Bois defended his family during the 1906 Atlanta Riot: He secured his family in their apartment and went to purchase a gun, and was prepared to use it. In "A Litany of Atlanta," he decried the violence and put this travesty of justice into historical context. In 1908, the Springfield Riot exposed white rampages as a national problem and not a Southern one. The nation's failure to prosecute the culprits in these atrocities implicated respected political and cultural institutions, which informed Du Bois's role in helping to establish the NAACP and its decision to organize against lynching and other forms of racist violence.

Unchecked racist violence continued. It included daily retaliations against those who resisted Jim Crow, reflected in lynchings and untold arrests in the expanding carceral state, which spurred the Great Migrations out of the South. Black migrants soon realized, however, they could escape the South, but not the violence.

Mass-killing sprees continued as whites instigated violence in Northern and Western cities where Southern transplants converged. In 1917, in East St. Louis, Illinois, after a labor dispute, whites attacked and killed Black residents. Thousands fled the city, heading towards the bridge connecting to St. Louis, where they were met by mobs and by police who closed the overpass. Desperate targets tried to swim across the Mississippi and many drowned. Officially, thirty-nine Black people were killed but, likely, there were more. In 1919, when Black people protested racial injustice or defended themselves, white mobs resorted to the same playbook in more than twenty-five cities and towns. African Americans fought back in all instances, but were often outnumbered.

Perpetrators paid no price for their crimes. The threat of reprisal kept many survivors from discussing what happened. Meanwhile, white supremacists and their apologists erased the history of these atrocities, and when they could not do that, they repeated the old script, exonerating the culprits and assuming no responsibility for stopping future violence.

Lynchings and mass killings eventually declined across the country, in the 1930s and 1940s, in response to economic and political pressure on the states. When businesses seeking to invest in the South raised questions about how secure their interests would be in states with unchecked mob violence, elected officials and chambers of commerce applied pressure to end it. There was an increase in federal officials committed to enforcing the due-process and equal-protection clauses of the Fourteenth Amendment. These officials were open to passing federal anti-lynching laws for states that refused to prosecute known lynchers, thereby eliciting the transformation of Southern governors, who had previously decried their powerlessness against the will of their white supremacist constituents. But white hate reared its head whenever Black people asserted their right to be free, feel safe, and participate in the democratic process.

The Civil Rights Movement saw a new wave of attacks that had not been witnessed since Reconstruction. The desegregation of public institutions, coupled with the recognition of Black people's voting rights, shifted the axis of the white power structure, giving rise to church bombings, the beatings of Freedom Riders and sit-in demonstrators, and the assassinations of movement leaders like Medgar Evers and Martin Luther King Jr. White antipathy for Black people's fight to be free and secure remained like a radioactive fog. The South still had terror groups, but through arrests and prosecutions, the federal government signaled it was ready to enforce African Americans' rights to due process and equal protection under the law.

WHITE SUPREMACY in America is structural, the result of centuries of policies and practices embedded in institutions. So, while extralegal violence was declining, extrajudicial violence was emerging as a new frontier, because many white Americans gave police a license to maim and kill Blacks in the name of preserving law and order.

Police officers had participated in lynchings, riots, and attacks on civil rights activists. And if state actors weren't active participants, their negligence implicated them in racist atrocities. The Black Panther Party made police violence a civil rights issue. Predictably, law enforcement retaliated and when Blacks protested, police, the media, and elected officials portrayed them as violent and lawless, justifying any violence against them.

Reform-minded police chiefs in cities like Washington, DC, thoroughly investigated shootings and prohibited officers from shooting at fleeing, nonviolent suspects. Restraint reduced the killings until the escalation of the so-called War on Drugs. When shootings rose in the 1990s, victims' families and the larger public were told by law enforcement that officers acted lawfully and their use of deadly force was justified. With no legal or political incentives to stop them, police became more brazen. Technological advancements allow police killings to be video recorded and posted on social media. Unfortunately, revelations of excessive force and police malfeasance have not changed the practices of authorities or the perspectives of juries.

Police killings, along with white vigilante violence, is what gave rise to the #BlackLivesMatter campaign that formed after the 2013 acquittal of a white supremacist who killed Trayvon Martin. One of the Movement for Black Lives' main objectives is to connect present-day violence to the past, so that Black people can be free and feel safe from white supremacy.

Reminders about the insecurity of Black life resurfaced in 2015, when a white man attended a bible study at Charleston's Emanuel African Methodist Episcopal Church and shot nine people to death. Because of the Lost Cause narrative and subsequent twisted tales erasing racist violence, many Americans could not see the connections between the 2015 killings and the violence that thwarted the

Bible owned by Polly Sheppard, survivor of the Emanuel AME Church massacre. A longtime member of Mother Emanuel, Sheppard had been in church business meetings all day on June 17, 2015. She did not plan to attend Bible study that night, so she left her Bible at home. Her friend, Myra Thompson, who was leading a study of the parable of the sower from the book of Mark, convinced her to stay. As one of only three people to survive the shooting, Sheppard continues to use this Bible for spiritual guidance, comfort, and strength.

President Barack Obama sings "Amazing Grace" at the funeral service for Rev. Clementa Pinckney, who was one of nine people murdered at Emanuel AME Church in Charleston, South Carolina, on June 17, 2015. The massacre at Mother Emanuel demonstrated that 150 years after emancipation, African Americans continue to face the threat of white supremacist violence in their daily lives. Black churches, as long-standing symbols of community, freedom, and empowerment, are often targeted for acts of racial terror.

promise that Reconstruction held. That the killer embraced the Confederate flag and the values associated with it was not lost on historians. They seized the moment to connect the present to the past, by launching the *Charleston Syllabus*, a crowd-sourced, social media campaign that made available historical records and scholarly research on the long history of anti-Black violence across the nation, including that used to overthrow Reconstruction.

The country appears to be on the cusp of a national reckoning concerning the lies told about Reconstruction, but the work remains unfinished. Reclaiming the history of how white terror undid Reconstruction fosters an understanding of the price African Americans paid for seizing their freedom. This reclaiming process also engenders a different viewpoint of current-day state violence and white supremacist acts. If Americans who believe in liberty and justice are to honor our national creed, then we, as a people, must stop the list of names from growing and see to it that African Americans are afforded the full protection of our democracy. Only then can we create a world where the Charleston shooter's victims—Rev. Depayne Middleton-Doctor, Cynthia Hurd, Susie Jackson, Ethel Lance, Rev. Clementa Pinckney, Tywanza Sanders, Rev. Daniel Simmons, Sharonda Coleman-Singleton, Myra Thompson—and other victims of state and vigilante violence would still be with us.

• • •

LEGACIES OF REPAIR

Katherine Franke

WHAT KIND OF INJURY to human dignity does enslavement inflict, and how should that injury be remedied? What is required to deliver enslaved people from a state of bondage to one of freedom? These difficult questions were richly debated in the 1860s and remain critical to contemporary efforts to provide reparative justice for slavery.

Nowhere was the failed promise of reparations more evident than in the Sea Islands of South Carolina. On November 4, 1861, the largest attack fleet ever to sail under the US flag was amassed to capture Port Royal, South Carolina. Confederate white islanders were outgunned and outmanned, and three days later nearly all of the local white men had packed their wives, children, and favorite "servants" into boats and left for the mainland. Federal troops immediately emancipated the Black people held in bondage and began a model program of reparations. When federal troops assumed

Family on Smith's Plantation, Beaufort, South Carolina, 1862. After gaining their freedom, African Americans on the Sea Islands sought to claim ownership of the lands they had cultivated during slavery. They knew that owning land was the key to full freedom and economic independence. For a brief time, the federal government supported their aspirations, but after the war ended, most of the land allocated to freed people was returned to its former owners.

control of the Sea Islands, approximately 10,000 Black people living on 189 plantations were immediately set free, two years before President Lincoln issued the Emancipation Proclamation.

The Black people of the Sea Islands did not passively wait to see how this new group of white people would govern their lives as freed people. Rather, they made their demands clear: "We want land and we want to build new lives apart from white people." The military and political leaders who were directly responsible for stewarding Black people from enslavement listened, and recognized that being set free without material resources would lock Black people into a permanent, intergenerational status of American peasantry.

Gen. Rufus Saxton led the military and humanitarian efforts in the Sea Islands, and was one of the most ardent advocates of land-based reparations. In his view, freed people held an equitable mortgage on the land, secured by their past, unpaid wages and sweat, blood, and lost lives. He felt that the enslaved people:

> *had been the only cultivators [of the land], their labor had given it all its value, [and] the elements of its fertility were the sweat & blood of the negro so long poured out upon it, that it might be taken as composed of his own substance. The whole of it was under a foreclosed mortgage for generations of unpaid wages.*

A teacher from Philadelphia who traveled to the Sea Islands, in the summer of 1862, to help educate freed people, echoed Saxton's views: "If there is any class of people in the country who have priority of claim to the confiscated lands of the South, it certainly is that class who have by years of suffering and unrequited toil given to those lands any value they may now possess." Saxton then put in place a process by which the freed people of the Sea Islands could make formal claims to the land, where property lines covered the same terrain as blood lines: The old plantation boundaries told Black people who their kin were.

As an initial matter, the freed people of the Sea Islands were promised that they should make claims to land there, and that title would be given to them as reparations for enslavement. Within days of learning of this promise, freed people overwhelmed the local land office, with claims to the property on which they and their ancestors had been enslaved, leaving cash deposits to signal their serious intent to own land. Officials began to issue "land certificates" to them, instructing them to begin building new lives on "their" land.

One group of freed people filed a claim for the Pleasant Point plantation, accompanied by a hand-drawn map that indicated how they would share the parcel as a community. In the days after filing the claim, they began to build cabins and plant provision crops on the property, taking concrete steps to create new lives as free people. The map was shaped by the natural topography of the area, bounded by "the pasture field," "the burying ground creek," and the "cut-off creek." Notably, recently freed Black women such as Mary Brown and Nancy Wilson received title to this property. Ironically, the freed women of the Sea Islands enjoyed greater rights than married white women of the era who could not own land in their own names. Nevertheless, formerly enslaved Black women in the Sea Islands were granted ownership by the federal government. These certificates are housed in the National Archives, bearing the *Xs* that freed people signed. Next to the *Xs* on these documents are ink imprints of hands, representing the formerly enslaved people of the Sea Islands engaging in their first acts of freedom, as "people." These *Xs* marked freedom from slaveowners' commands and signaled the change in their identity, from property to that of landowner. The documents described the newly freed people as "loyal citizens and heads of families," a radical recognition of their humanity.

Unfortunately, officials in Washington, DC, overruled local officials and ordered that the land be sold at two auctions. Ignoring these orders, local officials continued to issue land certificates to freed people, even as the land auctions began to take place. The Black people of the Sea Islands pooled their money to buy land at the auctions, but, for the most part, were outbid by white, Northern land speculators who swarmed to the Sea Islands to snap up land, financed by investors in Boston, New York, Philadelphia, and Pittsburgh.

Of the 20,000 acres that were sold in open bidding and ended up in private hands at the March 1863 auction, 2,595 acres were bought by freedmen and freedwomen. In the end, just over 1,000 Black families were able to buy land—a fraction of the freed people who had selected plots, planted crops, and made down payments.

The enterprise of providing freed people reparations in the form of land titles was tried a second time when, in January 1865, Union general William Tecumseh Sherman issued Special Field Order No. 15, setting aside a strip of coastline stretching from Charleston, South Carolina, to the St. Johns River in Florida, and into the mainland thirty miles from the coast. The order redistributed approximately 400,000 acres of land to newly freed Black families in forty-acre lots. On this land, Sherman ordered, "no white person whatever, unless military officers and soldiers detailed for duty, will be permitted to reside," and the freed people would be left to their own control. Sherman's order is the source of the demand still made today that Black people receive "forty acres and a mule."

Garrison Frazier, a newly freed sixty-seven-year-old man told General Sherman that Black people preferred to live alone, apart from white people, "for there is a prejudice against us in the South that it will take years to get over." Mr. Frazier also told the general, "[t]he way we can best take care of ourselves is to have land and turn it and till it by our own labor. . . . We want to be placed on land until we are able to buy it and make it our own." Others told Sherman: "What is the use of giving us freedom if we can't stay where we were raised and own our own house where we were born and our own piece of ground?"

This historic campaign for reparative justice came to an abrupt end after President Lincoln was assassinated and Andrew Johnson, a well-known slavery sympathizer, assumed the presidency of the United States. Johnson vetoed a bill from Congress that would have legislated the allocation of land to newly freed, Black people as reparations. He also granted amnesty to former Southern, Confederate landowners by signing an "Iron Clad Oath" that restored "all rights in property, except as to slaves." President Johnson dismissed the Sherman land titles, declaring them legally unenforceable.

To the U S Direct Tax Commissioners for the State of South Carolina.

The Undersigned, residents of Ladies Island loyal Citizens and heads of families hereby make application to preempt the following tracts of land in accordance with instruction of the President of the United States approved Dec 31. 1863. Said tracts being a part of the Pleasant Point plantation on Ladies Island and bounded & described as follows viz;

Cut off Creek

	Tom Gillison
	Adam Green
	Mary Brown
	Nancy Wilson
	Tom Gillison

North by Cut off Creek Easterly by Mulberry Hill Creek, Southerly by land taken up by Adam Green, Westerly by Black Horse Creek Containing twenty acres
Witness Geo H Hull   Tom Gillison his X mark

Northerly by land taken up by Tom Gillison Easterly by Mulberry Hill Creek Southerly by land taken up by Mary Brown, Westerly by Black Horse Creek. Containing twenty acres
Witness Geo H Hull   Adam Green his X mark

Northerly by land taken up by Adam Green Easterly by Mulberry Hill Creek & Flat Dam Southerly by land taken up by Nancy Wilson Westerly by Black Horse Creek & the pasture field. Containing twenty acres. Witness Geo H Hull   Mary Brown her X mark

Northerly by land taken up by Mary Brown, Easterly by Flat Dam, Southerly by land taken up by Tom Gillison, & Westerly the Pasture field, Containing twenty acres
Witness Geo H Hull   Nancy Wilson her X Mark

Northerly by land taken up by Nancy Wilson Easterly by Flat Dam & Burying Ground Creek Southerly by Burying Ground Creek & Westerly by the Pasture Field Containing twenty acres
Witness Geo H Hull   Tom Gillison his X Mark

Ladies Island January 29th 1864

Edisto Island S.C.

Oct 28th 1865.

To the President of these United States.

We the freedmen

Of Edisto Island South Carolina have learned
From you through Major General O O Howard commissi
oner of the Freedmans Bureau. with deep sorrow and
Painful hearts of the possibility of goverment restoring
These lands to the former owners. We are well aware
Of the many perplexing and trying questions that burden
Your mind. and do therefore pray to god (the preserver
Of all. and who has through our late and beloved
President (Lincoln) proclamation and the war made
Us A free people) that he may guide you in making
Your decisions. and give you that wisdom that
Cometh from above to settle these great and Important
Questions for the best interest of the country and the
Colored race: Here is where secession was born and
Nurtured Here is were we have toiled nearly all
Our lives as slaves and were treated like dumb
Driven cattle, This is our home, we have made
These lands what they are. we were the only true and
loyal people that were found in posession of these
lands. we have been always ready to strike for
liberty and humanity yea to fight if neede be
To preserve this glorious union, Shall not we who
Are freeman and have been always true to this
Union have the same rights as are enjoyed by
Others,? Have we broken any law of these United
States? Have we forfieted our rights of property
In land?—— If not then! are not our rights as
A free people and good citizens of these United States

Shortly after learning that the land they had been promised was being stolen from them and returned to their former enslavers, a group of freed people in the Sea Islands wrote to Gen. Oliver Otis Howard, a Northern officer appointed to head the newly created Freedmen's Bureau, insisting that he not implement this new policy, because "this is not the condition of really free men." They stated,

> General we want Homestead's; we were promised Homestead's by the government, If It does not carry out the promises Its agents made to us, If the government Haveing concluded to befriend Its late enemies and to neglect to observe the principles of common faith between Its self and us Its allies In the war you said was over, now takes away from them all right to the soil they stand upon save such as they can get by again working for your late and thier all time ememies.–If the government does so we are left In a more unpleasant condition than our former we are at the mercy of those who are combined to prevent us from getting land enough to lay our Fathers bones upon. We Have property In Horses, cattle, carriages, & articles of furniture, but we are landless and Homeless, from the Homes we Have lived In Landless. Homeless. Voteless. we can only pray to god & hope for his help, your Infuence, and assistance.

Thus, the land that had been set aside and granted to freed people to begin anew was seized from them, sometimes violently, and returned to their former owners, even though in many cases the formerly enslaved had paid for title to the land at public auction. Freed people were then forced to enter into years-long labor contracts with plantation owners who had previously owned them, and to work under conditions that bore a greater resemblance to slavery than to freedom. If they refused to sign these contracts, they were forced to leave the Sea Islands. The contract-labor system laid the ground for exploitive labor practices that followed in subsequent years, such as sharecropping. This is what being freed, but not free

A committee of freedmen on Edisto Island, South Carolina, sent this petition to President Andrew Johnson in October 1865, urging him not to return the land granted to them by the government to its former Confederate owners. "This is our home," they declared. "We have made these lands what they are." The committee also petitioned Gen. Oliver Otis Howard, commissioner of the Freedmen's Bureau, to support their claims as loyal and rightful owners of the land. (See Appendix B on page 202 for transcript.)

looked like for the formerly enslaved people of South Carolina. As W.E.B. Du Bois famously wrote, "The slave went free; stood a brief moment in the sun; then moved back again toward slavery."

In many cases, the white speculators who were the top bidders at the Sea Islands auctions that returned freed peoples' land titles to white people capitalized as much as or more than former Confederate plantation owners. These investors from the North bought at bargain prices plantations that their former Confederate owners never returned to claim. Even wealthy industrialists like Solomon Guggenheim bought plantations in the Sea Islands after the land had been divested from Black ownership.

Perhaps an even greater insult to the notion of reparative justice for formerly enslaved people was the passage and implementation of the Homestead Act in 1862. The law provided title to up to 160 acres of government land to any person who "improved" the plot by building a dwelling and cultivating the land. After five years on the land, the person could receive title to the property, free and clear, upon payment of a small registration fee. Thus, at the exact moment that the federal government considered, and then rejected, awarding land titles to freed Black people as reparations, land was being given away for free in the US West. Under the Homestead Act, 1.5 million families, almost all of whom were white, gained title to 246 million acres of land—almost 10 percent of all the land in the United States, as it existed during that period.

These land grants enabled self-reliance, freedom, and the accumulation of generations of wealth for white people. In 1995, a government agency reported that forty-six million people—about a quarter of the US adult population—were descendants of people who received land under the Homestead Act. "Upward mobility, economic stability, class status, and wealth"—values that figure so prominently in the myth and reality of the American Dream— were realized through "one national policy—a policy that in practice essentially excluded African Americans," observed Professor Thomas M. Shapiro in his book *The Hidden Cost of Being African American: How Wealth Perpetuates Inequality*.

NEARLY 7 MILLION BLACK PEOPLE were legally enslaved in this country. Their enslavement was the foundation for the early political and economic enterprise of this nation. Historian Walter Johnson, in a *New York Times* op-ed, in March 2013, wrote, "The labor of enslaved people underwrote 19th century capitalism. Enslaved people were the capital: four million people worth at least $3 billion in 1860 . . . was more than all the capital invested in railroads and factories in the United States combined." The United States Constitution embraced and rested upon the institution of slavery, and slavery helped the United States evolve from a colonial economy to the biggest industrial power in the world.

The ongoing demands for reparations in the United States are grounded in the fact that, while the institution of slavery may have been formally abolished in the 1860s, enslaved people never received any kind of remedy to heal the rape, torture, death, and destruction of millions of human souls. The demands are also a recognition that

John Summer residence near Dunlap, Kansas, ca. 1880s. In the late 1870s, as conditions grew worse for African Americans in the South under white Democratic rule, many decided to seek better opportunities elsewhere. The desire to own homesteads drew migrants to the Great Plains, where they established "colored colonies" in places like Dunlap, Kansas; Boley, Oklahoma; and Sully County, South Dakota. But unlike their white counterparts, Black homesteaders faced discriminatory laws and practices that blocked their efforts to acquire good land and build wealth.

THE MAURY COUNTY EX-SLAVE CONVENTION

H. DICKERSON   MRS. CALLIE HOUSE

Ex-Slave Mutual Relief, Bounty & Pension Association

WILL CONVENE AT

Columbia, Tenn., March 24th to 27th, 1899.

....

Every ex slave and friend is cordially invited to take part in this great and
grand work. Come and exchange views one with the other upon the great ques-

Founded in Nashville, Tennessee, in 1898 by Callie House and Isaiah Dickerson, the Ex-Slave Mutual Relief, Bounty and Pension Association was part of an early nationwide reparations movement. The organization lobbied Congress to provide pensions for formerly enslaved African Americans, based on the model of pensions issued to US military veterans. It also served as a mutual-aid society, offering insurance and burial assistance benefits. By the end of 1899, the group had 34,000 members.

being set free without material resources locked Black people into a permanent intergenerational status of American peasantry. Individual slaveholders profited greatly, but were never required to disgorge the profits they made, nor did they have to retroactively compensate enslaved people for the theft of their labor, safety, families, dignity, and lives. In actuality, former slaveowners were compensated generously for their lost land and property with US tax dollars. For example, in one county in the Sea Islands of South Carolina alone, the US Treasury tracked down and paid former plantation owners a total of $207,166.58 ($5,927,035.85 in 2020 dollars) for the land they lost during the Civil War. Thus, white slave-owners were ultimately "made whole" for any costs they may have incurred from seceding from the Union and siding with the losing, proslavery cause.

Over the centuries, racial-justice advocates, such as Frederick Douglass and Queen Mother Audley Moore, made the case for reparations. In 1881, Frederick Douglass wrote,

> *When the Hebrews were emancipated, they were told to take spoil from the Egyptians. When the serfs of Russia were emancipated, they were given three acres of ground upon which they could live and make a living. But not so when our slaves were emancipated. They were sent away empty-handed, without money, without friends and without a foot of land on which they*

Our wives, our children, our husbands, has been sold over and over again to purchase the lands we now locates upon. For that reason we have a divine right to the land. . . . And then didn't we clear the lands and raise the crops of corn, of cotton, of tobacco, of rice, of sugar, of everything? And then didn't them large cities in the North grow up on the cotton and the sugars and the rice that we made? Yes! I appeal to the South and to the North, if I hasn't spoken the words of the truth. I say they have grown rich, and my people are poor.

—BAYLEY WYAT, speech at meeting of freedmen near Yorktown, VA, 1866 *could live and make a living. Old and young, sick and well, were turned loose to the naked sky, naked to their enemies.*

US Representative John Conyers Jr. introduced a bill in every Congress for nearly thirty years to study the institution of slavery and to recommend appropriate reparations. These demands finally gained mainstream attention in the past several years. Representative Conyers's bill finally got a hearing in 2019. Additionally, a number of cities and towns have enacted laws creating reparations, and churches, universities, and private companies have implemented reparations policies.

So, what is meant by reparations, why might they be owed, who should get them, what form should they take, and should someone or some group be expected to give up something as part of a reparations plan? Two competing proposals for cash payments to Black Americans have been developed. One side insists that the descendants of enslaved people are most deserving of cash-based reparations, and have calculated that a federal expenditure of $10.7 trillion, or $267,000 per person, should be paid to the 40 million eligible, Black descendants of slavery. Other proponents of reparations do not advocate limiting reparative justice only to those who can show a lineage to an enslaved person, but that all Black people are impacted by the legacy of slavery in the United States.

Reparations should not be understood as taking one form. Current examples illustrate how reparative justice for slavery and the badge of inferiority that white supremacy has inflicted on Black people in this country can, and should, be responsive to the contexts and histories in which the call for reparations has taken hold. Such contexts and histories can include addressing issues such as educational and economic inequities.

Georgetown University, a Jesuit institution, is an example of reparations in the educational realm. In 1838, the Jesuit priests who ran Georgetown University sold 272 men, women, and children to pay its debts. The university gained roughly $3.3 million in today's dollars from this sale. In 2016, the university began a process of

developing reparations for that horrendous sale. This has included an apology from university leaders and a program by which the school would provide admission, free tuition, and a special fund for the descendants of the 272 people sold. Students at Georgetown continue to push the university to do more. Virginia Theological Seminary, Princeton Theological Seminary, Brown, Columbia, Harvard, the University of Virginia, Smith College, and other institutions of higher learning have undertaken similar, reparative initiatives to address their relationship to slavery. Calls have also been made for reparations to include the full funding of historically Black colleges and universities.

Attempts to correct past historical injustices and inequities in home ownership were the focal points for the City Council in Asheville, North Carolina. In July 2020, it voted unanimously to remove a Confederate monument that was erected on the site of slave auctions.

In 1989, Rep. John Conyers Jr. of Michigan introduced a bill in Congress to study the issue of reparations for slavery. The bill proposed to establish a commission to "examine the institution of slavery, subsequent de jure and de facto racial and economic discrimination against African Americans, and the impact of these forces on living African Americans," and to recommend "appropriate remedies." Conyers continued to introduce a version of the bill in every session of Congress until he retired in 2017.

Census document listing the names and ages of the enslaved men, women, and children, "272 in all," sold from Maryland Jesuit plantations in 1838 to pay the debts of Georgetown University. After the university launched an initiative in 2015 to examine its institutional ties to slavery, these individuals became known as the Georgetown University 272 (GU272). The GU272 Descendants Association was founded in 2016 to unite and advocate for families whose ancestors were enslaved by the Society of Jesus.

The initiative also funded programs that help increase homeownership and business and career opportunities for Black residents. Providence, Rhode Island, and the former Confederate capital, Richmond, Virginia, have taken steps to follow Asheville's lead.

In June 2019, the City Council of Evanston, Illinois, established a reparations fund from the revenue generated from the legal sale of cannabis, and in March 2021 Evanston became the first city in the United States to adopt a specific, reparative-justice plan to address discrimination against its Black residents, including a program to subsidize Black homeownership.

The history of Black people being freed, but not provided with any resources to establish individual or collective economic stability, let alone family wealth, goes a long way in explaining the stark, racial wealth gap today: The net worth of a typical white family is nearly ten times greater than that of a Black family. The average Black household would need 228 years to accumulate as much wealth as its white counterpart holds today. Also, despite the passage of federal and local laws, in the 1960s, prohibiting race-based discrimination in housing, education, and employment, "virtually no progress has been made over the past 70 years in reducing the wealth inequality between Black and white households," observed researchers at the Federal Reserve Bank of Minneapolis, in a report from 2018. Something more than passing laws prohibiting race discrimination must be done to address the long-term reality of the racial wealth gap.

Community land trusts (CLTs) have emerged as another transformative form of repair. The underlying philosophy of the early CLTs reflected a notion that "land is treated as a common heritage, not as an individual possession," and prioritized housing as a right, not a commodity that is bought and sold in a market that is subject to speculation, gentrification, and price gouging. CLTs transfer resources and property into Black communities and empowers them.

Mélisande Short-Colomb (*above*) was one of the first two GU272 descendants admitted to Georgetown University in 2017. She is a descendant of Abraham Mahoney and Mary Ellen Queen, two enslaved people sold by the Jesuits in 1838. On campus, Short-Colomb cofounded the GU272 Advocacy Team to raise awareness and lobby for restorative justice. She wore this button (*opposite bottom*), printed with her ancestor's name, during a 2019 student referendum campaign for a tuition fee to benefit GU272 descendants.

Nia Umoja and Takuma Umoja stand in front of their garden in Jackson, Mississippi, with their daughter, Zola Selassie, and family friend, Mosi Selassie, in 2016. The Umojas founded the Cooperative Community of New West Jackson as part of a grass-roots initiative to develop independent and sustainable Black urban communities through cooperative land ownership. These contemporary efforts to address economic injustice also evoke cooperative strategies used by newly freed African Americans during Reconstruction to acquire land, build communities, and promote self-sufficiency.

Jackson, Mississippi, provides an interesting case study for how racial-justice advocates use CLTs as a form of reparations for historic and systemic race discrimination. The Fannie Lou Hamer Community Land Trust, a project of a community network called Cooperation Jackson, echoes the land-redistribution project that took place in the Sea Islands. The trust has purchased nearly forty lots in West Jackson, a working-class, predominantly Black, underdeveloped neighborhood not far from the downtown capital district. Most of the land the trust has purchased was acquired through state tax auctions that occurred pursuant to a Mississippi law that permits the confiscation of land with over three years of unpaid taxes.

The trust's plan is to build and run housing for the community as a self-sustaining collective. Collectivized ownership and energy independence, relying heavily on solar power, are designed to hold off gentrification, displacement, and housing vulnerability for the working-class and poor members of the community. As one of the founding members of Cooperation Jackson, Sacajawea "Saki" Hall, puts it: "We're not about getting in on the American Dream, we want to get beyond individual ownership of property. We want control of our own dreams."

Racial-justice activists in Jackson have developed a political program to implement a reparative vision of the city. This vision is grounded in a commitment to cooperative, bottom-up, democratic governance, and includes the creation of community land trusts and "freedom farms"—urban, worker-owned, cooperative farms that would produce organic vegetables for the community.

The modern ownership structures developed in Jackson echo the spirit of the experiments in freedom in the immediate aftermath of the Civil War in the Sea Islands and other locations. In both contexts, community and land ownership were organized collectively; healing and empowerment of the community were premised on independence from the larger white society; land was seen as a community resource to share rather than to exploit for individual profit or investment; and the safety and health of the community were premised upon land being held in the community's name and interest.

Land has always played a critical role in the civic ideal of freedom in this country. When asked at the 2020 Black National Convention, "Why is it essential that land is a part of our strategy for Black people to build power?" Rev. Wendell Paris Sr. declared, "Land is the basis of all wealth, land is the basis of power, land is the basis of independence. If you're looking to becoming free and liberated, you need to figure out your relationship to the land."

What enslaved people got when they were emancipated was freedom on the cheap. The dangling *d* at the end of "free" stood as a kind of residue of enslavement that bound them to a past, and marked their future as free*d*, not free, people. The *d* served as a racial mark that structured the kind of freedom formerly enslaved people received as something less than that with which white people were endowed as a matter of natural, or God's, law.

Author Toni Morrison (*far left*) led a procession in 2008 to dedicate a memorial bench on Sullivan's Island, South Carolina, where enslaved Africans were quarantined upon their arrival in North America. The Bench by the Road Project, an initiative launched by the Toni Morrison Society in 2006, installs black steel benches as symbolic sites of remembrance. These memorials serve, in Morrison's words, to "summon the presences of, or recollect the absences of" enslaved people who were erased from history.

The promise and the failure of reparations in the 1860s has animated the current call for reparations, not necessarily or only in the form of individual cash grants, but through collective resource redistribution. Just as the dangling *d* differentiates a free*d* people from the truly free people, the dangling *s* of reparation*s* bears witness to multiple forms of repair that may be necessary to bring about real justice for slavery. For this reason, advocates insist that structural, comprehensive, and ongoing reparations are required to address the wounds of the past and ameliorate an enduring social, political, economic, and legal identity of freed people as something less than white people. The idea that reparations for slavery were owed to formerly enslaved people, and that the debt remains outstanding, is by no means a radical, modern notion, as the history of the Sea Islands shows us. Today's emerging embrace of the moral imperative of granting reparations for slavery to Black people renews that unanswered call. Contemporary demands for reparations are premised on the notion that the past has enduring moral relevance today, and that slavery, while legally abolished, continues to reverberate through American culture, so we should make amends for that past. The speech made by Martin Luther King Jr. at the March on Washington on August 28, 1963, drew from the idea that a debt was still owed to Black people for slavery. King said,

> *We've come to our nation's capital to cash a check. When the architects of our Republic wrote the magnificent words of the Constitution and the Declaration of Independence, they were signing a promissory note to which every American was to fall heir . . . . It is obvious today that America has defaulted on this promissory note insofar as her citizens of color are concerned. Instead of honoring this sacred obligation, America has given the Negro people a bad check, a check which has come back marked "insufficient funds."*

Most white people have never really considered what it meant to be enslaved or to have had one's ancestors enslaved, and then to be emancipated into a state of abject poverty, as were Black people in the United States. Instead, Black people are asked to believe that they can have a piece of the (white) American dream, if they work hard enough.

Reparative-justice mechanisms, such as apologies and memorials, in addition to monetary reparations, could have the effect of forcing a national reckoning that would compel all Americans to identify with the experience of slavery in the United States, while owning its legacy as part of our past and present. At a minimum, we owe this kind of recognition and remembrance to the freed people who were promised so much and given so little. Black lives will continue to be treated as though they do not matter until we take meaningful steps to repair the intergenerational wreckage that slavery inflicted on Black people.

• • •

Century Plant 85 Years old.

Seabrook's Plantation.

LEGACIES OF PLACE

Mary Elliott

EDISTO ISLAND is twenty-five miles south of Fort Sumter, South Carolina, the Civil War's ground zero, where shots were fired in April 1861. The island is profoundly significant to the story of Reconstruction, because this is where African Americans engaged in a historic fight for post-enslavement land distribution, arising from the promise of forty acres and a mule. It is the site from which the Point of Pines slave cabin was acquired for the National Museum of African American History and Culture's *Slavery and Freedom* inaugural exhibition. Edisto Island is also the site of another historically important place: The Hutchinson House, situated near the original Point of Pines cabin site, symbolizes the intertwined legacies of two families—one Black, one white—that seek to reconcile their common ancestry born during the era of enslavement.

ARLENE ESTEVEZ, A BEAUTIFUL, dark-skinned woman with piercing light eyes, was a descendant of the enslaved African American people who transformed Edisto Island through generations of blood, sweat, and tears. Carroll Belser, a white woman, had the same build and similar light eyes as Arlene, and descended from one of the island's largest white enslaving families.

On a hot spring day on Edisto Island, Arlene was intent on keeping Carroll at arms-length. Carroll wanted to talk about their common lineage and learn about her African American relatives. Arlene was passionate about family history, but was not ready to discuss her potential white ancestral connections. Like many African Americans descended from enslaved Black women and their enslavers, such lineage most often resulted from nonconsensual relationships. Weighty issues of race, identity, gender, and enslavement gave Arlene pause. However, she realized that Carroll may have had key information regarding her enslaved ancestors. So, she agreed to meet with Carroll at her plantation-style home on the water, where Carroll revealed that their common relatives were Isaac Jenkins Mikell, a white enslaver, and Jim Hutchinson, an enslaved black man, whose mother was an enslaved black woman. After a glass of wine, Arlene told Carroll about her side of the family, and that her brother, Greg, was researching and writing a family history. Carroll shared that she contributed to the published genealogy of her side of the family, as she handed Arlene a copy of the book and requested to receive a copy of Greg's completed book. Generations after the abolition of slavery, and only a few years after Arlene and Carroll's first encounter, these two branches of one family reunited as they gathered around their shared ancestral site—the Hutchinson House, which still stands today. It represents Arlene, Greg, and Carroll's connection through slavery, it represents slavery writ large, and it represents the meaning of freedom.

On the same day Arlene and Carroll met, they had participated in the community effort to preserve the history of the Point of Pines slave cabin, which was built in the early 1850s. The Edisto Island Preservation Society helped facilitate the donation of the

Point of Pines slave cabin on Edisto Island, South Carolina, as it appeared in 2013. Built in 1853 to house enslaved plantation workers, this 16 ft. x 20 ft. cabin continued to serve as a home for generations of African American families until the 1980s. Today, the preserved cabin is the centerpiece of the *Slavery and Freedom* exhibition at the National Museum of African American History and Culture, where the many layers of its history are revealed and shared with the public.

cabin from the descendants of the enslaving family to the Museum. Over the course of a week, the slave cabin was meticulously taken apart in preparation for its conservation and ultimate placement in the Museum's *Slavery and Freedom* inaugural exhibition. Through the Museum's community collecting effort, a more inclusive history of Edisto Island was constructed. Every day during the dismantling process, community members, including longstanding residents and descendants of enslaved African Americans and white enslavers, came together at the site, sharing stories that broadened the historical purview. Their insights added nuance to the community story that is part of a larger American story. The gathering was a kinship reunion as much as it was a recovery of history.

The story of the Point of Pines plantation begins with Paul Grimball, a merchant from England, who arrived with his wife and daughters in 1674 in colonial Charles Towne (modern-day Charleston) South Carolina, where he owned six hundred acres. By 1683, he had acquired 1,590 acres of land, as one of the first Edisto Island residents to receive a headright land grant—that is, land given to colonists as an incentive, and increased based on the number of indentured servants and enslaved people the colonists transported to the colony. Grimball brought with him several European indentured servants, adding to his growing colonial enterprise. Together with Grimball, they began to clear the land, build improvements, and plant seventy acres of corn. Grimball also secured livestock from the English colony, Barbados. He named his homestead along the North Edisto River Point of Pines.

In 1684, Spanish colonists from Spanish Florida and the African people they enslaved attacked the Edisto Island area and destroyed the original Grimball homestead, including a river-front home made of tabby, the ruins of which can still be seen today. A determined Paul Grimball relied on the forced labor of enslaved people of African descent to rebuild his home. It is believed that Grimball's earliest purchase of enslaved people from Barbados occurred between 1684 and 1685. He also purchased many people as they arrived directly from West Africa. At least 40 percent of captive Africans enslaved in North American colonies came through South Carolina ports. In 1732, Edisto planters collectively owned 546 enslaved people of African descent. While the trans-atlantic slave trade tried to strip them of their African heritage, their assigned names, such as "Angola Jack" or "Gamboa George," often hint at homelands, which connect them to their traditions, cultures, languages, and faiths spanning the continent of Africa.

Grimball amassed wealth as a landowner from the commodities produced by enslaved laborers and from his investment in human capital (enslaved African people). Such wealth afforded Grimball a great deal of influence and power. He served as the secretary of the colony under five different governors, having held the position from 1684 until his death in 1696. He bequeathed Point of Pines to his family, and his heirs passed their legacy of wealth, power, and influence on to succeeding generations.

In 1789, the Grimballs sold their property to the Bailey family. By 1792, taxes on enslaved people exceeded land taxes and provided funding for the colony. Around 1853, Charles Bailey erected the Point of Pines slave cabin along a row of at least ten other cabins, among the pines and directly across from the fields, creating what is known

The ache for home lives in all of us,
the safe place where we can go as
we are and not be questioned.

—MAYA ANGELOU, *All God's Children Need Traveling Shoes*, 1986 as a slave street. Before the Civil War, there were 170 enslaved African Americans at Point of Pines who generated wealth for their enslaver by cultivating Sea Island cotton. In the late eighteenth century, enslaved African Americans comprised 60 percent of the Edisto population. By the nineteenth century, there was a Black majority of 90 percent.

The Bailey family were members of Trinity Episcopal Church. They are listed in church records, along with several Black people they held in bondage. Down the road, the Edisto Island Presbyterian Church, attended by many of Edisto's most-prominent, elite planter families, also included a "slave gallery" composed of several twenty-foot-long pews that lined the upper level of the church. An obelisk featured on the church grounds marks member contributions of money and "slaves." Enslaved men, women, and children that were donated to the church were known as the pastor's "parish slaves." They were forced to work for the support, comfort, and prosperity of the pastor. Edisto Island Presbyterian Church ultimately served as the site where formerly enslaved African Americans claimed their humanity, their right to the ownership of land and their own labor, marking their claim to true freedom.

Rev. Edward Thomas, an itinerate pastor, noted in his records, "July 1827 Baptized a colored child by the name William. Parents William Simmons, a freeman and Dido a slave." Such unions were tenuous since they were under the control of the enslavers. Most plantations were managed by an overseer and/or an enslaved driver. Enslaving families were often absent, which provided a small measure of autonomy for enslaved laborers and enabled the creation of the Gullah culture. The Gullah language blends Anglo-English, Arabic, and multiple African languages, and is still spoken today. Enslaved and free people of African descent also retained and passed on traditional African foodways, worship and burial practices, and music and dance styles. Examples include Hoppin' John, a dish composed of rice and peas, and Red Rice, a dish cooked in tomato sauce. The activity referred to as "seeking" is a religious rite of passage. The Ring Shout is a holy dance with Arabic origins. It is performed in a

Balcony pew (*right*), from Presbyterian Church (*above*), ca. 1876 on Edisto Island, South Carolina. After white residents fled the island in 1861, in advance of US troops, freed people held their own worship services in this church, led by a Black minister. They also established a school at the church. In 1866, white members returned and reclaimed ownership of the building. Rather than go back to the segregated balcony, the Black congregants left and established a new church, which they named Edisto Presbyterian Church.

Group of men, women, and children at Cassina Point Plantation, Edisto Island, South Carolina, 1862. During the Civil War and Reconstruction, the newly freed residents of Edisto Island laid claim to the lands that their families had cultivated for generations. They established their own communities based on kinship networks, cultural traditions, and a strong sense of place. They also transformed the landscape by building farms and homesteads, schools, churches, and other institutions to support and secure self-determination.

counterclockwise motion that includes foot stomps, accompanied by call-and-response vocalizing.

Despite the inhumane conditions that enslaved people endured, including violence, physical strain, and mental abuse, they held on to their humanity. Their toil transformed the land into a place of beauty. They loved one another, built kinship communities, practiced their faith, and held on to the hope of freedom. Deceased enslaved people were buried at various sites across the island, connecting the living to the ancestral land. For the most part, families remained intact. Loved ones who did not work on the same plantation were usually enslaved on nearby plantations.

ABRAHAM LINCOLN was elected president in November 1860. Leading up to the election, slavery was a priority concern of many enslaving states. By December, South Carolina seceded from the Union citing a list of reasons, but the issue of slavery was the first and foremost cause of the Civil War in 1861.

Two years before Lincoln signed the Emancipation Proclamation, seventy-four enslaved people—the majority women—escaped from Cassina Point plantation near Point of Pines. In November 1861, as war activity drew closer to Edisto Island, the Confederacy informed enslaving families there that they had to abandon their homesteads immediately and leave "their property" behind, including land and enslaved men, women, and children. When the enslavers vacated, Black people experienced an odd form of freedom because they were still, legally, in bondage but self-governing until the Union Army arrived in February 1862. Several Union Army troops occupied various plantations on the island and set up their command center at Point of Pines plantation. Subsequently, Union Naval forces were sent to retrieve the remaining African Americans from the island and take them to Beaufort, South Carolina, as contrabands of war, or confiscated Confederate "property." The 1,600 relocated Black Edistonians became part of the Port Royal Experiment, whereby the United States created schools and hospitals for African American Sea Islanders and allowed them to buy land and farm plantations abandoned by Confederate owners. The formerly enslaved longed to return to the site they considered home and sought to be reunited with the landscape they transformed under enslavement—where they also created home and community despite their condition.

There were others who forged their own paths to freedom. William Bailey and Jim Hutchinson were among the formerly enslaved African Americans who evaded the Union Army roundup and removal to Beaufort. The two men eventually made contact with the Union Navy. Hutchinson escaped capture from Confederates who had set up an outpost near Edisto Island. He served as an informant for the Union Navy and, in so doing, was able to assist in the capture of nine Confederate officers of Company I of the Third

South Carolina Cavalry, including one by the name of Townsend Mikell Hutchinson—Jim Hutchinson's cousin. Hutchinson ultimately enlisted with the Union Navy and served from 1863 until his discharge at the end of the war in 1865.

In January 1865, Congress passed the Thirteenth Amendment, ending slavery in the nation. Almost a year later, it was ratified. The same month the amendment was passed, Union general William Tecumseh Sherman issued Special Field Order No. 15, which provided that 400,000 acres of confiscated and abandoned Confederate land would be distributed in forty-acre plots to formerly enslaved African American men and women. It also provided for loans of mules. In addition to the land, Order No. 15 encouraged Black men to serve in the Union military during the war. President Lincoln established the Bureau of Refugees, Freedmen, and Abandoned Lands in March 1865, known as the Freedmen's Bureau. A month later, the war ended when the Confederate states surrendered. Shortly thereafter, President Lincoln was assassinated and replaced by his vice president, Confederate sympathizer Andrew Johnson.

Reconstruction had begun and the effort to reunite the country was underway. Eventually, the Confederate states were brought back into the Union and African Americans transitioned into society as free people. For many Black people, the need to reunite with family was paramount and also served communal needs, because family and kinship networks strengthened the effort to survive and build upon their free status. Newly freed people placed ads in various publications, including the *Christian Recorder*. Polly Fields hoped to reconnect with her mother through the following ad: "Information Wanted of My Mother, three sisters and brothers. My mother's name is Rose Jackson; sisters, Peggy Endona, Susan and Nancy Jackson. My brother's name, John Miles. My sister, Endona and I were sold 28 or 30 years ago in the speculators' house in Charleston, S. C., to Frank Threadwell. —Polly Fields, Eufaula, Ala., care Rev. J. E. Fields."

In addition to reconstituting family and kinship networks, ownership of land was of utmost importance to formerly enslaved

used to belong to Jackson Talley and was bought by Mr.
Wright, Boydtown, C. H. You will please send the enclosed
letter to my sister Jane, or some of her family, if she
is dead — I am, very respectfully,

your obedient servant,
Hawkins Wilson —

Dear Sister Jane,

Your little brother Hawkins is trying to
find out where you are and where his poor old mother
is — Let me know and I will come to see you — I shall
never forget the bag of biscuits you made for me the
last night I spent with you — Your advice to me to meet
you in Heaven has never passed from my mind and
I have endeavored to live as near to my God, that if He saw
fit not to suffer us to meet on earth, we might indeed
meet in Heaven — I was married in this city on the 10th March
by 1867 Rev. Samuel Osborn to Mrs. Martha White, a very intelligent
and lady-like woman — You may readily suppose that I was
not fool enough to marry a Texas girl — My wife was from
Georgia and was raised in that state and will make me
very happy — I have learned to read, and write a little — I teach
Sunday School and have a very interesting class — If you
do not mind, when I come, I will astonish you in religious
affairs I am sexton of the Methodist Episcopal church—colored
I hope you and all my brothers and sisters in Virginia will
stand up to this church; for I expect to live and die in
the same — When I meet you, I shall be as much
overjoyed as Joseph was when he and his father met

people. Land allowed for self-sufficiency, self-improvement, and the fulfillment of self-determination. Land provided a place to build homes, places of worship, schools, and businesses. It provided a place to plant crops and provisioning gardens, to earn money and support families. The formerly enslaved of Edisto Island demanded access to the land that they cultivated and made profitable—where they worshipped under the trees in the hush harbors (secret sites for religious meetings) and where their ancestors were buried. They claimed abandoned land and sought education, citizenship, and voting rights.

Garrison Frazier was a Baptist minister who gained his freedom after sixty years of enslavement. A designated leader among a group of Black religious leaders, his words resonated with General Sherman when the two men met just before Order No. 15 was issued. Frazier stated that freedom meant "placing us where we could reap the fruit of our own labor and take care of ourselves . . . to have land and turn it and till it by our own labor."

The Point of Pines cabin and several other cabins still stood in a row across from the fields of cotton and among the pines, when returning formerly enslaved African Americans petitioned for land and began to create their new lives. Gen. Oliver Otis Howard was designated to oversee the operations of the Freedmen's Bureau. In July 1865, Howard issued Circular No. 13 confirming freedmen's right to confiscated and abandoned land, but General Sherman's forty acres and a mule decree had no permanency: The land that was promised had been distributed to and taken away from the newly freed at least twice. Compounding the problem, President Andrew Johnson received petitions from former Edisto Island enslavers seeking to regain ownership of their plantation homes. The petitioners considered it "cruel and unjust to separate them from their ancestral homes, their communities and church homes where their ancestors were buried." The president pardoned the former Confederates and assured them that their property would be returned to them. In September 1865, President Johnson demanded that General Howard rescind the land offer and issue Circular No. 15, directing the restoration of land to the former owners.

The following month, in October 1865, nearly 2,000 Black men and women took time out from building their community to listen to a message from General Howard at the Edisto Island Presbyterian Church. Every pew was full and it was quite a scene when the Black people gathered learned that the land promised to them would be returned to their former enslavers. Several attendees shouted "No!" as the crowd erupted. Witness accounts state that an elderly African American woman settled the crowd as she began to sing "Nobody Knows the Trouble I've Seen" and others joined in. General Howard asked that the group of formerly enslaved people "lay aside . . . bitter feelings and reconcile . . . with former masters." A committee of freedmen responded to Howard in a letter dated October 21, 1865, and stated,

> we want Homesteads; we were promised . . . by the government . . . we are at the mercy of those who are combined to prevent us from getting land enough to lay our Fathers bones upon.
> You ask us to forgive the land owners of our Island. . . . The man who tied me to a tree & gave me 39 lashes & who stripped and flogged my mother & my sister . . . I cannot well forgive."

While some freedmen were able to secure small tracts of land, the majority of the Black population was forced by circumstance into sharecropping contracts with the tenuous promise of a share of the profits. They moved into former slave cabins, including the cabins at the Point of Pines plantation. They purchased necessities on credit and hoped to secure their share of the profits at the end of the season in order to avoid debt, but they were often cheated and wound up in debt peonage, another form of enslavement.

FORMER US COLORED TROOPS MEMBER, Jim Hutchinson, returned to Edisto and was recognized in the Black community as a war hero. He established himself as a leader and organizer, much despised by the white residents. He served as an Edisto Island

Henry Hutchinson and his wife, Rosa, raised their family on Edisto Island, South Carolina. They owned and operated a cotton farm as well as a cotton gin that served the community of Black farmers on Edisto until the 1930s.

Republican precinct chair and organized interracial alliances to vote in local, state, and national elections. Hutchinson formed a co-op to secure 900 acres of land on the island. In 1868, he acquired 400 acres of land on Point of Pines Road, not far from the site of the cabin. He ultimately divided the property among his children and a few other African American residents as they worked to reconstitute a Black community—this time unencumbered by slavery.

Jim Hutchinson was an outspoken, confident, established, and effective leader among the Black freedmen and freedwomen on Edisto Island. He was devoted to truth and unity between the races. His hopes for a progressive future came to an end when he was murdered in 1882 by a white man. Hutchinson's son, Henry, carried on his father's legacy. In 1882 he had an African American artisan design and build a home for his new bride, Rosa, on the land left to him by his father. The home came to be known as the Hutchinson House. Henry, like his father, was successful. He was one of two Black cotton-gin owners on Edisto.

Succeeding generations of African American descendants of Jim Hutchinson served as stewards of the family homestead. The plantations on Edisto Island are centuries old, but this is the oldest

African American-owned structure. It has good bones and the heart of it just needs to be revived. Ultimately, the last family steward put the ancestral home on the market. The Edisto Island Open Land Trust stepped in and purchased the home, preventing the sale to a private individual. The Land Trust is working to preserve the historic site, with support from the Hutchinson descendants and local residents. The College of Charleston's American College of the Building Arts is also assisting with the historic-preservation effort.

The Hutchinson House on Edisto Island, South Carolina, as it appeared around 1900. Henry Hutchinson built this house in 1882 on land acquired by his father, Jim Hutchinson. The house, which still stands today, symbolizes the island's legacies of family, land, and freedom.

The Hutchinson House was saved from demolition through the unyielding efforts of community members, including Gretchen Smith, executive director of the Edisto Island Historic Preservation Society, and John Girault, executive director of the Land Trust. Smith, a beloved member of the community, is deeply rooted in Edisto and steeped in the history of the island. She recognized the exigent circumstance with the Hutchinson House and immediately coordinated with the Hutchinson descendants and local residents. Girault stepped in and was able to secure a loan for the Edisto Island Land Trust to purchase the house. Once the house is restored, there are plans to use it as a site to teach the history of Edisto Island and the African American community. Girault consults with Arlene's brother, Greg Estevez, and his extensive community network to ensure the integrity of the project, which has received widespread media coverage and important funding. Like the slave cabin, the Hutchinson House serves as a prompt for audiences to reflect on the history of Edisto Island, Point of Pines, slavery and freedom, as well as the humanity and important contributions of African American people to the nation.

Smith helped to secure the Point of Pines slave cabin. She and genealogist, Toni Carrier, facilitated conversations and meetings between museum curators and the descendant community members, including descendants of enslaved African Americans who lived in the cabin and descendants of the white enslavers who owned Point of Pines plantation.

The community-collecting effort regarding the slave cabin and the restoration of the Hutchinson House engages diverse audiences. The interracial and intergenerational effort can only make local communities stronger and make the nation better. Community members are also confronting the history of race and racism, as they gather for public programs about the local history and engage in organic, and sometimes challenging, conversations between friends and family. They give each other space to share their stories and hear one another; to recover the shared and inclusive history; and to work together to repair the wounds born out of a dark past. The Hutchinson House serves as a reminder of the hard-fought battle of formerly enslaved African Americans to stake their claim in the nation they helped create.

GREG ESTEVEZ finally published his family history in which he quotes Edisto Island historian and author, Charles Spencer, who states, "African American families and their lives on Edisto, is a story yet to be told systematically and in depth. I sincerely hope someone will take up the task soon. We all need to hear it." In Greg's personal reflections of his multiyear journey to tell the history, he recounts how he sat with his cousins, Emily Meggett, an esteemed elder on Edisto Island whose husband grew up in the Point of Pines cabin, and Carroll Belser. He shared how they energized his desire to share more aspects of the story.

One can hope that Arlene was present in spirit at the gathering with Greg, Ms. Emily, and Carroll. The woman with the beautiful brown skin, piercing light eyes, joyful spirit, and strong commitment to family and her kinship community, died one month before the highly anticipated grand opening of the Smithsonian National Museum of African American History and Culture. She was

surrounded by family when she passed, including her cousin, Carroll. The two women formed an unbreakable and undeniable bond. They cultivated a sincere and loving friendship that transcended race and enabled a meaningful descendant reunion. Greg, Gretchen Smith, and Carroll represented Arlene well at the Museum's grand-opening donor event. They saw the Point of Pines slave cabin featured at the heart of the Museum. It tells the unvarnished truth of slavery and Reconstruction. It also speaks to the humanity and resilience of African Americans and transmits the legacy of place. It is considered one of the Museum's and the nation's treasured objects.

• • •

Emily Hutchinson Meggett (*left*) and Isabell Meggett Lucas (*right*) visit the Point of Pines slave cabin at the National Museum of African American History and Culture in 2017. Lucas, daughter of Catherine and Gussie Meggett, was born in the cabin on Edisto Island in 1930. She and other members of the Meggett family shared memories of the house. "No one ever called it a 'slave cabin,'" said Lavern Meggett, Lucas's great-niece. "It was just a place we called 'home.'"

LEGACIES OF BELIEF

Hasan Kwame Jeffries

NINE MINUTES AND TWENTY-NINE SECONDS is a long time to kneel. It is an especially long time to kneel on someone's neck, but that is exactly how long a white Minneapolis police officer knelt on the neck of George Floyd, a forty-six-year-old Black man. For nine minutes and twenty-nine seconds, the officer pinned Floyd to the ground, ignoring his cries of "I can't breathe" and disregarding his pleas for mercy. For nine minutes and twenty-nine seconds, the policeman slowly suffocated Floyd until life finally left him. The unfathomable cruelty of the officer's act and the callous indifference of the three other patrolmen, who watched without intervening, shocked and outraged people across the globe. A video of the May 25, 2020, murder went viral immediately. Within days, millions took to the streets in the largest demonstrations in US history, and millions more marched in solidarity throughout the world.

The Daughters of the Confederacy has placed
a plaque here, at the fort's entrance—
each Confederate soldier's name raised hard
in bronze; no names carved for the Native Guards—
2nd Regiment, Union men, Black phalanx.
What is monument to their legacy?

—NATASHA TRETHEWEY, "Elegy for the Native Guards," 2007

The protesters issued three demands.

First, they wanted justice for Floyd. They called on prosecutors to arrest and charge the officers with murder. They also wanted justice for several other African Americans who had recently been murdered, including Breonna Taylor, who was shot in her sleep by police in her Kentucky home just two months earlier, and Ahmaud Arbery, who had been stalked and murdered in cold blood by three white men in Georgia one month before that.

Second, they demanded public affirmation of Black humanity, insisting that the names of the victims of racial terror be spoken, because their lives and their deaths deserved to be acknowledged. They also urged people to say "Black lives matter" and reminded them to do so by painting murals across the nation, featuring the simple, yet poignant, three-word affirmation.

And third, the protesters wanted the truth to be told about America's past. They recognized that systemic racism cannot be eliminated if people do not understand the origin and evolution of systems and structures that maintain inequality. To this end, they rallied behind longstanding calls to remove monuments that perpetuated false narratives about American history, especially the several hundred Confederate statues situated throughout the South.

Richmond, Virginia, the former capital of the Confederacy, quickly emerged as the focal point of efforts to remove monuments celebrating white supremacy. After Reconstruction, supporters of the Confederacy embarked on a campaign to restore the city to its antebellum standing. Central to this plan was the construction of a boulevard of monuments commemorating notable Confederates, anchored at one end by a twelve-ton equestrian statue of Robert E. Lee, the commander of the Army of Northern Virginia. Black Lives Matter protesters in Richmond appealed to lawmakers to remove the statues lining Monument Avenue, but a lawsuit initiated by white residents prevented immediate action. In response, activists reclaimed the space, occupying the grassy area surrounding the statue and holding spirited demonstrations every day for weeks. They also reimagined the statue itself, covering it with political slogans condemning racism and affirming Black humanity, while artists projected onto it images of Black freedom fighters, including abolitionists Harriet Tubman and Frederick Douglass.

Two months after Floyd's murder, his family joined the Richmond protesters for the unveiling of a hologram honoring his life. The memorial consisted of pin-dot laser lights, flittering about in front of Lee's statue, that suddenly came together to create a stunning portrait of Floyd. "We're here to share this special moment," said Rodney Floyd, George's brother, adding, "Right now, right here, this is a beautiful scene."

The determination of Black Lives Matter protesters to remove and replace Confederate monuments, and the insistence of Confederate sympathizers to retain the statues, reflect competing understandings of the present, and contrasting visions of the future. These differences also reflect conflicting beliefs about the Civil War and Reconstruction. The two opposing sides are not merely at odds over the interpretation of a common set of facts, they are at odds over the existence of fundamental facts.

For those protesters who transformed Lee's statue into a memorial for racial justice, their knowledge of the Civil War and Reconstruction was rooted in reality. They were aware that slavery was the cornerstone of the Confederacy and that preserving the institution was the primary cause of the Civil War. They knew that the Confederate generals Robert E. Lee, and Stonewall Jackson, and President of the Confederate States, Jefferson Davis, immortalized in bronze and stone, were enslavers of Black men, women, and children who took up arms against the federal government. They recognized that Reconstruction was a legitimate attempt by the party of Lincoln to extend basic civil and human rights to African Americans, an effort that resulted in extending the franchise to Black men. They knew these established truths because Black folk had been taught them as far back as Reconstruction, in the Black public schools that Black legislators created when they ushered in the South's first public education systems.

But, for those who insisted that the monuments remain, their knowledge of the Civil War and Reconstruction was based on a web of lies spun shortly after these eras ended. They believed in the mythology of the Lost Cause. This tale holds that the Civil War was a valiant crusade to preserve a noble way of life unrelated to maintaining slavery. It asserts that Reconstruction was a misguided social experiment brought about by massive federal overreach and highlighted by unprecedented political corruption. Worse still, the earliest iterations of the Lost Cause framed slavery as benign, enslavers as beneficent, the enslaved as content, and racial-terror groups, such as the Ku Klux Klan, as chivalrous defenders of white womanhood.

Although fabricated from whole cloth, the mythology of the Lost Cause gained popularity in the wake of Reconstruction because of a propaganda campaign led by the United Daughters of the Confederacy (UDC). Stitched together in 1894 by weaving a loose network of local Confederate memorial organizations, the UDC promoted the Lost Cause, indoctrinating white youth through its pro-Confederate educational materials and programs.

The UDC's 1904 *Catechism for Children* asked its readers, "What causes led to the war between the States, from 1861 to 1865?" and answered, "The disregard, on the part of the States of the North, for the rights of the Southern or slave-holding States." It also asked, "What were those rights?" and stated plainly, "The rights to regulate their own affairs and to hold slaves as property." Although the UDC conceded that slavery was a primary factor in causing the war, it assured readers that enslavers were helpful and that the enslaved were happy. The question, "How were the slaves treated?" was answered, "With great kindness and care in nearly all cases." The *Catechism* went on to ask, "What was the feeling of the slaves towards their masters?" replying, "They were faithful and devoted and were always ready and willing to serve them."

Adopting the same method used by Christian churches to teach religious doctrine, the United Daughters of the Confederacy's catechism presented questions and answers about Confederate history for children to memorize and recite. These texts, first published in the early 1900s, provided a blueprint for constructing belief in the legitimacy of the Lost Cause. Line by line, generation by generation, they built up a mythical Southern past untainted by historical realities of racial injustice, terror, and brutality.

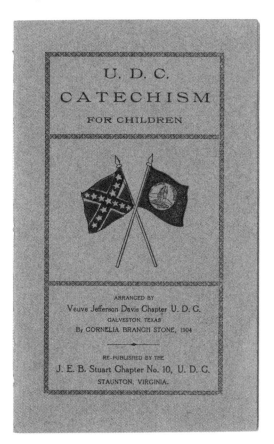

The UDC promoted the Lost Cause to an even wider audience by insisting that schools adopt text-books that reflected the ahistorical view that it had concocted. The UDC's North Carolina Division pledged in its constitution to make sure that "the portion of American history relating to [the Civil War] shall be properly taught in the public schools of the State, and to use its influence towards this object in all private schools."

Julian Carr, a North Carolina industrialist and avowed white supremacist, lent his support to this effort by helping lead the Rutherford Committee, a small group of representatives from Confederate propaganda organizations that dedicated itself to promoting the Lost Cause through textbooks. Formed in 1919, the committee published *A Measuring Rod to Test Text Books, and Reference Books in Schools, Colleges and Libraries*, a twenty-three-page pamphlet that newly formed state textbook commissions used to decide which books to allow in schools. If the committee discovered an objectionable textbook in a classroom, the book was banned and those responsible for introducing it were fired.

These Confederate propagandists were not professional historians, but they received the backing of academics through the work of Columbia University historian and political scientist, William Dunning. Dunning and his acolytes argued in their histories of Reconstruction, which were among the very first to be written, that Confederates were honorable, Radical Republicans were ignoble, African Americans were ignorant, racial terrorism was understandable, and segregation was inevitable. For Dunning, who was quoted in *The Atlantic*, the great misstep in Southern history was not slavery, but rather Reconstruction, which he argued attempted to force "the coexistence in one society of two races so distinct in characteristics as to render coalescence impossible." This conclusion found its way into popular histories of the period, as well as into textbooks. One widely read US history survey written by historian James Ford Rhodes claimed: "The scheme of reconstruction pandered to ignorant Negroes, the knavish white natives, and the vulturous adventurers who flocked from the North."

Along with textbooks, the UDC spearheaded the drive to place Confederate propaganda in schools. In the 1930s, the North Carolina Division distributed two hundred portraits of Confederates to be hung in classrooms, along with more than a thousand Confederate flags.

The UDC also led the movement to erect monuments celebrating the Confederacy, eventually littering the landscape with inexpensive, mass-produced statues and obelisks. The locations that they chose were not random. The sites were purposefully selected to convey that these were spaces where white supremacy prevailed. Often placed in town squares or outside of county courthouses, these monuments signaled to African Americans that they would find neither justice nor peace. Instead, they would find all-white juries who refused to convict whites for crimes they committed against African Americans, and refused to find African Americans not guilty of crimes they had not committed.

Efforts to inscribe Lost Cause beliefs into the built environment came in two waves. The UDC spearheaded the initial push, which took place during the first two decades of the twentieth century, paralleling the rise of Jim Crow—the system of legal segregation that defined the color line for a full century after emancipation. This wave featured the installation of most Confederate monuments and memorials.

The UDC received support for its work in 1915 with the release of D. W. Griffith's *The Birth of a Nation*. The three-hour, silent film was an ode to the Lost Cause. It depicted slavery as a positive, Reconstruction as a disaster, and the Klan as heroes. It also brought Vaudeville minstrelsy to the silver screen by drawing on racial stereotypes of Black people, who were portrayed in the film by actors in blackface. Despite its virulent racism (or more likely because of it), *The Birth of a Nation* became Hollywood's first blockbuster, earning tens of millions of dollars. The film had a natural audience in white Southerners, who had been fed a steady diet of Lost Cause propaganda for years. But it also found an enthusiastic audience of white Northerners, despite blaming them for the Civil War and belittling them for subjecting the South to post war "Negro rule." President

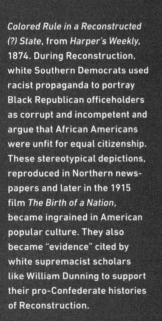

Colored Rule in a Reconstructed (?) State, from *Harper's Weekly*, 1874. During Reconstruction, white Southern Democrats used racist propaganda to portray Black Republican officeholders as corrupt and incompetent and argue that African Americans were unfit for equal citizenship. These stereotypical depictions, reproduced in Northern newspapers and later in the 1915 film *The Birth of a Nation*, became ingrained in American popular culture. They also became "evidence" cited by white supremacist scholars like William Dunning to support their pro-Confederate histories of Reconstruction.

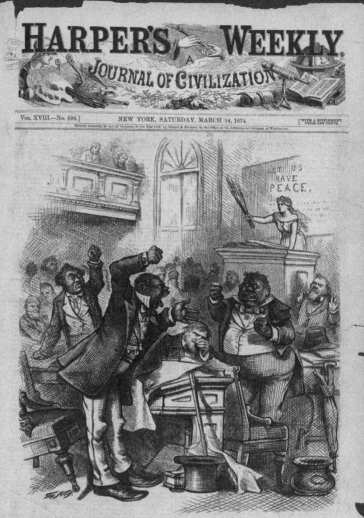

Woodrow Wilson, who instituted racial segregation in the federal government, hosted a private screening of the film at the White House and afterward sang its praises.

The trigger for the second wave of public memorials was the Civil Rights Movement of the 1950s and 1960s. In 1954, the US Supreme Court ruled that segregation in education was unconstitutional, infuriating white supremacists. Adding Confederate symbols to state flags and renaming things was one way segregationists registered their opposition to the ruling. Led by state legislatures, this surge was evident throughout the South. The Georgia General Assembly added the Confederate battle flag to Georgia's state flag in 1956. South Carolina was among the Southern states that chose not to change its flag. Instead, in 1961, it hoisted the Stars and Bars above its capitol, where it flew alongside the American flag and the Palmetto flag. Mississippi did not do anything: It had already added the Confederate cross to its flag in 1894. This period also saw the renaming of roadways and schools after Confederate leaders. Seemingly, every Southern state now had a Jefferson Davis or Dixie Highway.

Flooding public spaces with Confederate propaganda has kept the Lost Cause visible to this day. This twisted history can be seen in the bronze, equestrian statues that loom large in parks in Charlottesville, Virginia, and in the massive, bas-relief sculpture at Stone Mountain in Georgia. Lost Cause symbols can also be viewed in the hallways of Robert E. Lee High School in Jacksonville, Florida, and along Confederate Avenue in Baton Rouge, Louisiana. The memorial drinking fountain at the county courthouse in Wilson, North Carolina, and the lone soldier standing sentry outside the Clarendon County courthouse in Manning, South Carolina, are clear reminders of a distorted history, as is the playing of "Dixie" under Friday night lights by the Refugio, Texas, high school marching band.

Confederate apologists insist that Lost Cause propaganda is simply an expression of cultural heritage, a celebration of the "southern way of life." This has led seven state legislatures to pass laws to prevent the removal of Confederate monuments and memorials. In May 2017, Alabama governor Kay Ivey signed the Alabama Memorial

Preservation Act, prohibiting local governments from touching monuments located on public property that had been in place for more than forty years. But the movement launched over a century ago by the UDC to install Confederate monuments and memorials in public places was hardly an innocent act of regional pride or civic virtue. It was a concerted effort to impose a set of beliefs about the Civil War and Reconstruction that reinforced white supremacy.

When the UDC began its propaganda campaign, white supremacist political violence was rising, and, to justify their actions, the perpetrators of racial terror pointed to the growing catalogue of myths about Reconstruction, including the mistaken notion that the politics of the period were inherently corrupt. In 1898, in Wilmington, North Carolina, white Democrats warned of an impending return to "Negro Rule" that they insisted had taken place during Reconstruction. In response, a mob of several thousand whites invaded the coastal city, killing scores of African Americans, forcing Republican elected officials to resign, and marching Black political leaders out of town at gunpoint with instructions never to return. The coup d'état effectively ended Black political participation in Wilmington for three generations.

On the campus of the University of North Carolina at Chapel Hill, in 1913, the same beliefs about Reconstruction that had animated white rioters in Wilmington were expressed by those who had gathered on campus to dedicate a memorial to the Confederacy. Julian Carr, the Southern industrialist, thanked the UDC for the gift of a bronze statue of a Confederate soldier, which would come to be called "Silent Sam." Carr heaped praise on those who wore the "old Grey" for what they "meant to the welfare of the Anglo Saxon race" during Reconstruction, when "the bottom rail was on top, all over the Southern states." He said, "Their courage and steadfastness saved the very life of the Anglo Saxon race in the South," and "today, as a consequence the purest strain of the Anglo Saxon is to be found in the thirteen Southern States." Carr went on to boast that shortly after Lee's surrender at Appomattox, and not far from the spot where they stood that day, he "performed the pleasing duty" of

In 2017, the Washington National Cathedral removed two stained-glass windows honoring Confederate generals Robert E. Lee and Stonewall Jackson that had been installed in 1953. The removal was prompted by the massacre at Emanuel AME Church in Charleston, South Carolina, and the Unite the Right rally in Charlottesville, Virginia. These events drew national attention to the embrace of Confederate symbols by white supremacists. The National Cathedral initially removed the Confederate battle flags, before deciding to remove the entire windows.

Confederate Memorial Day ceremony at Arlington National Cemetery, 1917. In 1864, the War Department established a cemetery for US soldiers on the confiscated plantation of Confederate general Robert E. Lee. Fifty years later, the United Daughters of the Confederacy dedicated a memorial on the same grounds to those who had taken up arms against the United States. A dramatic victory for the Lost Cause, it recast the Civil War as a story of white heroism, not Southern treason or Black liberation.

"horse-whipp[ing] a negro wench until her skirts hung in shreds." Her offense, he claimed, was having "publicly insulted and maligned" a white woman.

A full century after the dedication ceremony for "Silent Sam," white supremacists rallied on another Southern college campus— the University of Virginia. They came together under the guise of preventing the removal of Confederate statues in Charlottesville. During their rally, echoes of Carr's Lost Cause racism, filtered through the prism of anti-Semitism and Nazi propaganda, could be heard in their chants of "Jews will not replace us" and "Blood and soil." And the same violent impulses that animated rioters in Wilmington were on display as well, resulting in the murder of anti-racist counterprotester, Heather Heyer.

AFRICAN AMERICANS did not let Confederate propaganda go unchallenged. They recognized it for what it was—a deliberate attempt to spread misinformation about the Civil War and Reconstruction in order to justify racial inequality in the past and in the present.

When *The Birth of a Nation* was released, Boston-based activist, William Monroe Trotter, organized a grassroots campaign of marches and demonstrations to have it banned. The Black Harvard graduate and outspoken advocate of equal rights knew that, on average, at least one African American had been lynched every week for forty years, and the "murderous, cowardly pack," as the poet Claude McKay called them, typically justified their actions by claiming the victim had sexually assaulted a white woman. Trotter argued, therefore, that the film's depiction of Black men as depraved rapists would trigger white animosity and endanger Black lives. As such, the film was a threat to public order. But Boston's censor board, which had banned far less incendiary material, rejected Trotter's appeal. By 1915, narratives of the depredations of Reconstruction and the righteousness of the Klan had filtered North, and a shared belief in white supremacy rendered this implausible take on history believable.

The storming of the US Capitol on January 6, 2021, by a mob of President Donald Trump supporters, in an attempt to stop the certification of the election results, recalled the political violence of the Reconstruction era. Many of the insurrectionists brandished Confederate flags, along with other racist and anti-Semitic symbols. This man walks in front of a portrait of abolitionist and civil rights champion Sen. Charles Sumner.

While Trotter challenged the Lost Cause in popular culture, his Harvard classmate, the scholar-activist W.E.B. Du Bois, took on this mythology in academia. As early as 1903, in *The Souls of Black Folk*, his classic text of essays on race in America, Du Bois challenged the idea that Reconstruction failed because of Republican corruption and Black incompetence. Instead, he pointed to deliberate attempts by white Southerners to maintain slavery by other means, especially debt peonage. For the next three decades, despite the dogged attempts of white Southerners to undermine racial equality, Du Bois researched and wrote about Reconstruction, detailing the accomplishments of African Americans. Du Bois's work culminated in his magnum opus, *Black Reconstruction in America: An Essay Toward a History of the Part which Black Folk Played in the Attempt to Reconstruct Democracy in America, 1860–1880.*

Published in 1935, *Black Reconstruction* was a remarkable achievement, unsurpassed at the time in terms of depth and breadth of research, despite its heavy reliance on published public documents. *Black Reconstruction* exposed all that was wrong with the Lost Cause narrative and Dunning's analysis of Reconstruction. "We have spoiled and misconceived the position of the historian," wrote Du Bois. "If we are going, in the future . . . to be able to use human experience for the guidance of mankind, we have got to clearly distinguish between fact and desire. . . . I write then in a field devastated by passion and belief."

But Du Bois's truth telling wasn't enough. For years, Black folk read it, but white folk did not. Indeed, his work was dismissed by academic gatekeepers. The *American Historical Review* refused to review it. This was a part of a larger pattern and practice of disregarding attempts to set the record straight. "No amount of revision can write away the grievous mistakes made in this abnormal period of American history," wrote E. Merton Coulter in *The South During Reconstruction*.

Dismissive responses to critiques of the Lost Cause disappointed and frustrated African Americans, and the resurgence of Confederate propaganda during the Civil Rights Movement only

We have spoiled and misconceived the position of the historian. If we are going, in the future . . . to be able to use human experience for the guidance of mankind, we have got to clearly distinguish between fact and desire.

—W.E.B. DU BOIS, *Black Reconstruction in America,* 1935

intensified these sentiments. But these feelings did not prevent African Americans, in the past and present, from challenging the Lost Cause or the presence of its material representations in public.

In 1999, the NAACP, the nation's oldest civil rights organization, launched an economic boycott against the state of South Carolina, hoping to persuade lawmakers to remove the Confederate flag from atop the state capitol. The NAACP urged people not to vacation in the state, and called on entertainers and sports organizations, including the National Collegiate Athletic Association (NCAA), the leading body for college athletics, to avoid holding events in the state. The following year, the South Carolina legislature relocated the flag to a specially designated site on the capitol grounds. The NAACP was unimpressed. They continued the boycott for another fifteen years, until the flag finally came down after a white gunman, who viewed the Lost Cause as his own, massacred nine African Americans at Emanuel African Methodist Episcopal Church in Charleston, South Carolina. The NAACP drafted a resolution announcing the end of the boycott, calling the flag "a symbol of racial, ethnic, and religious hatred, oppression, and murder which offends untold millions of people." The resolution also noted that although removing the flag was "clearly a victory for the NAACP and a defeat for promoters of hate . . . there are still battles to be fought in other states and jurisdictions where emblems of hate and oppression continue to be celebrated." One such place was the campus of the University of North Carolina at Chapel Hill.

"Silent Sam," the Confederate statue that Julian Carr had dedicated in the name of white supremacy, had stood for a century, defended by university administrators and protected by campus police. In recent years, Black students led the charge to remove it, pointing to Carr's embrace of white supremacy as evidence of the ill intent of those who had gifted it. The continued failure of administrators to act led students to topple the statue in August 2018. "It was really a joyous moment," said Jasmin Howard, a twenty-eight-year-old alumna who was present when the monument finally came down.

W.E.B. Du Bois (*standing, right*) and staff in the offices of *The Crisis*, the journal of the NAACP. Du Bois served as founding editor of *The Crisis* from 1910 to 1934. Under his leadership, the monthly magazine became a major platform for civil rights advocacy, political commentary, and promotion of African American history and culture.

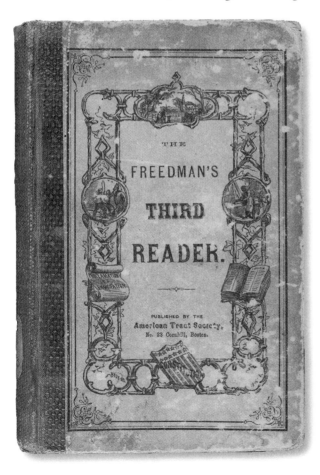

African Americans understood that the removal of Confederate statues and flags would not lift anyone out of poverty, but they also knew that it was important to rid public spaces of symbols that celebrated white supremacy and encouraged racial violence. While African Americans endeavored to eliminate public displays of objects of hate, they continued long-standing efforts to reclaim Reconstruction. For as long as the UDC has been working to rewrite Reconstruction, African Americans have been fighting for an honest account. This undertaking reflected their widely held belief that truth was a prerequisite for liberation.

Education was the focus of Black efforts to tell the truth about Reconstruction. From the moment slavery ended, African Americans organized to gain access to schools, flooding the Freedmen's Bureau with petitions identifying specific needs and requesting support. An appeal, dated August 17, 1867, came from Oak Hill in Granville County, North Carolina. Written by the district's "Colored Citizens" on behalf of "nearly sixty col'd children from ten to sixteen years of age," the petitioners explained that they would gladly send the young people to school "if a suitable building and teacher could be furnished."

In 1870, when Black men gained the right to vote under the Fifteenth Amendment, they leveraged the franchise to elect Black state legislators who enacted public education laws. These state statutes laid the groundwork for the first public education systems in the South. Although nearly all of the public schools established at this time were segregated, and very few pushed beyond the elementary grades, they still created space for African Americans to learn honest accounts of the past. In

Freedmen's school in North Carolina, ca. 1868. As freedom spread across the South during the Civil War, demands for education followed. The first "freedmen's schools," which educated girls and boys as well as adults, were established by Northern missionaries in areas occupied by the US Army. Newly freed African Americans soon began building their own community schools, often as part of churches, with teachers and supplies provided by the Freedmen's Bureau and Northern aid societies.

Jacksonville, Florida, African Americans invested in the segregated Edwin M. Stanton school, which, in the 1880s, graduated such young scholars as James Weldon Johnson, who in 1900 wrote the lyrics to "Lift Ev'ry Voice and Sing," the African American national anthem. In this same spirit, African Americans in Washington, DC, established the M Street High School, which emphasized academic and college preparatory subjects. M Street prepared Black students for a life of the mind, rather than a life in a field or factory.

It was at this time that most HBCUs were founded—thirty-four, in fact, between 1865 and 1877. Many were established by church organizations. The African Methodist Episcopal Church, the first Black independent Protestant denomination, opened Paul Quinn in Austin, Texas, in 1872, and a half dozen others over the years. Many of these schools, such as Morehouse College, which began in 1867 as Augusta Institute, aimed to prepare students to become ministers and missionaries as well as teachers. At its founding, neighboring Spelman College, which started out as Atlanta Baptist Female Seminary, adopted the motto "Our Whole School for Christ." The emphasis on molding minds and saving souls led to partnerships with white Protestant organizations and denominations, such as the American Missionary Association, which helped launch Atlanta University in Georgia, and the United Church of Christ, which started several schools, including Fisk University in Tennessee.

The focus on Christian training reflected African Americans' deep and abiding belief that academic education was inseparable from moral and spiritual education, and inextricably linked to civic education. This mindset predisposed African Americans to teach inconvenient truths about the opportunities gained and lost during Reconstruction when the Lost Cause narrative began to take hold.

Carter G. Woodson, who started what would become Black History Month, dedicated his professional life to researching and teaching the African American experience. In 1915, he helped found the Association for the Study of Negro Life and History, to illuminate African American contributions to American society, and in

Carter G. Woodson with issues of *The Negro History Bulletin*, ca. 1948. Known as the Father of Black History, Woodson dedicated his career to eradicating myths and misconceptions about the achievements of African Americans. Woodson created Negro History Week (the forerunner to Black History Month) in February 1926, choosing the date to coincide with African American traditions of commemorating the birthdays of Frederick Douglass and Abraham Lincoln.

1937, he launched the *Negro History Bulletin*, to help educators teach Black history accurately and effectively.

African American educator Nannie Helen Burroughs had a similar vision. In 1908, she founded the National Training School for Women and Girls in Washington, DC. Although she structured the school's curriculum to prioritize the industrial sciences, she also required students to study Black history. For Burroughs, instilling in her pupils an appreciation for those who fought for freedom during slavery and Reconstruction was just as important as teaching them a job skill.

African Americans' commitment to reclaiming Reconstruction was just as strong outside of the classroom. Fueled by the same truth-telling impulse, they celebrated the transition from slavery to freedom. In Gallipolis, Ohio, a hamlet on the banks of the Ohio River, African Americans have been celebrating Emancipation Day continuously since 1863. In Galveston, Texas, Black communities have celebrated Juneteenth, the day when word finally reached those enslaved in Texas that the Jubilee had finally arrived. And for quite a while, Black Bostonians came together to mark the ratification of the Fifteenth Amendment.

Black newspapers covered these community events from the start. And by the middle of the twentieth century, Black magazines such as *Ebony* and *Jet* published articles and essays that focused explicitly on countering false historical narratives like the Lost Cause. Lerone Bennett Jr., the long-time executive editor of *Ebony*, wrote a series of articles on the Black experience that served as the basis for his books *Before the Mayflower* and *The Shaping of Black America*.

African Americans have traditionally run toward history unafraid of what they might find, seeking out what others have tried to hide. Conversely, Confederate propagandists have been running from history, seeking to hide what others have been trying to find, afraid of the truths that might be revealed. The traditional African American approach to knowledge and understanding has become an essential part of Black culture. It has been taught by Black educators and has been celebrated by the Black community. It has also become a core component of Black protest movements, reflected most recently in the demands of Black Lives Matter protesters to remove Lost Cause idolatry from public spaces.

The Confederate tradition of promoting nostalgia over history has been woven into the fabric of American culture and has consequences far beyond historical misinterpretations. The promulgation of white supremacist beliefs led to ropes around the necks of Black people in 1920, and knees on the necks of Black people in 2020.

Reconstruction, therefore, has produced two legacies of belief, one white and the other Black. The white legacy, embodied by the Lost Cause, is fundamentally about miseducation. It is responsible for a fictionalized version of the past that has proven incredibly difficult to shake. It continues to occupy public space in the form of monuments, memorials, flags, and street names. It continues to be taught in schools, creating another generation of students who are ill informed about the past and ill prepared to confront the challenges posed by systemic racism and persistent inequality in the present. And it continues to reinforce white supremacy, fueling those driven by hate.

The Black legacy of belief, exemplified by Du Bois's *Black Reconstruction*, is centered on education for liberation. It is what motivated Black families in Oak Hill, North Carolina, to petition the Freedmen's Bureau for a schoolhouse. It is what inspired William Monroe Trotter to attempt to shut down screenings of Hollywood's first blockbuster. It is what informed the NAACP's decision to boycott South Carolina until it took down the Confederate flag. It is also what led Black Lives Matter protesters in Richmond to reinterpret the Lee monument after the murder of George Floyd. The Black legacy is responsible for a true accounting of the past. And although this body of thought has yet to emerge as the dominant public perspective, it has supplanted the cult of the Confederacy among professional historians.

The fundamental promises of Reconstruction, which included unfettered access to the ballot box and safety from racial terrorism, remain unfulfilled. And they cannot be fulfilled if people do not know what these promises were or why they have not been realized.

To meet today's challenges, we must confront the hard history of yesterday. But the white legacy of belief, centered as it is on nostalgia for the Confederacy, is incapable of pointing the way forward. Historical fabrications are not helpful. In fact, they are harmful because they obscure rather than reveal the causes and effects of racial inequality.

The Black legacy of belief, which illuminates Black lives, is a roadmap for revealing the truth about Reconstruction. It is a guide for distinguishing fact from desire. As such, it provides a blueprint for making sense of the present—for understanding the problem of racial inequality, the persistence of Black protest, and the possibilities of democracy. The time to follow its directions is now.

• • •

Celebrate and Commemorate Freedom, light projection at the National Museum of African American History and Culture, November 2015. Opened to the public in September 2016, the Museum created an unprecedented space for presenting Black history on a national scale. Its mission, in the words of renowned historian John Hope Franklin, is to "tell the unvarnished truth" about the past in order to help all Americans better understand the present and map a pathway to a more just future.

ACKNOWLEDGMENTS

Make Good the Promises: Reclaiming Reconstruction and Its Legacies is a work of remembrance and honor for the Reconstruction period, one of the most complex, misunderstood, and supremely significant periods of American history. It is a companion volume to the exhibition *Make Good the Promises: Reconstruction and Its Legacies*. Both represent the National Museum of African American History and Culture's continued exploration of the core narrative of slavery and freedom, central to the Museum's mission to present the American story through an African American lens. Realizing a task of such significance was dependent on the assembling of an exceptional array of scholars, editors, designers, and other professionals.

We are indebted first to the contributors to this volume, a distinguished group of historians, scholars, and educators whose critical knowledge of the period and its modern consequences brilliantly animate these pages. We thank Kimberlé Williams Crenshaw, Mary Elliott, Candra Flanagan, Katherine Franke, Thavolia Glymph, Hasan Kwame Jeffries, Kathleen M. Kendrick, and Kidada E. Williams for their remarkable and illuminating insights. We offer a special word of profound gratitude to Eric Foner, author of the book's foreword and the premier scholar on the Reconstruction period. His guidance has been invaluable to the Museum's development. Smithsonian secretary and founding NMAAHC director, Lonnie G. Bunch III, was the original champion of the exhibition and publication, and we thank him for this support. Director Emeritus Spencer R. Crew, preface author and one of the exhibition's cocurators, was a stalwart advocate throughout and is due our deepest gratitude.

This publication marks another milestone in the Museum's work with our stellar colleagues at Smithsonian Books. We are extraordinarily grateful to have worked on this singular publication with colleagues who have collaborated on a library of publications that have added to the literature on African American history and culture. Director Carolyn Gleason's keen editorial gifts and production acumen were critical in honing the content, design, and overall realization of the book. Our heartfelt thanks to senior editor Jaime Schwender whose unfailing diligence and generosity lifted our work at every step, and assistant editor Julie Huggins for her research and editorial support. A very special word of thanks to Gary Tooth of Empire Design Studio whose evocative and elegant design set the perfect tone for the publication. We also offer our immense gratitude to editor Karen D. Taylor for her deft navigating and honoring of the diverse voices of an array of writers.

We offer special thanks to the indefatigable Doug Remley, for his knowledge, research, recommendations, and ideas and for identifying the distinctive images that so aptly augment the narrative. Our sincere gratitude goes to the other members of our publications team, Danielle Lancaster and Jaye Linnen.

Kudos to our other museum colleagues, especially Kevin Young, Andrew W. Mellon Director, whose support helped make this publication possible. We extend our appreciation to Carlos Bustamante, Dorey Butter, Ruthann R. Uithol, Constance S. Beninghove, Emily Houf, Joseph A. Campbell, Mike Biddle, Jeannine Fraser, Shrita Hernandez, Gretchen Beasley, Eric Dixon, John Lutz, Adam Martin, Fleur Paysour, Debora Scriber-Miller, Taima Smith, Tiffanie Warner, the Museum's Cataloging and Digitization Team, and to all who contributed their insight and acumen at key moments to bring this publication to life.

I offer my deepest gratitude to my coeditor Paul Gardullo. His devotion to and depth of knowledge of African American history has never been more vividly evident as in this publication and the larger project, including his role as project director on the companion exhibition. His nuanced articulation of the contours of this vexed subject was irreplaceable. His passion, compassion, and thorough scholarship were bulwarks of our work together.

We also acknowledge with gratitude our literary agent, Marie Dutton Brown, for her wise counsel, and our publisher, Tracy Sherrod, of Amistad for being a supportive partner in this remarkable journey.

Finally, we are in debt to Frederick Douglass and all the courageous women and men, historical and contemporary, who endured extraordinary challenges and faced unimaginable obstacles, with unerring devotion, to insist that America make good on the promises of her Constitution. Their legacy persists in these pages and in the lives, laws, institutions, and communities of this nation.

—**Kinshasha Holman Conwill, Coeditor**

APPENDIX A

Thirteenth, Fourteenth, and Fifteenth Amendments to the United States Constitution

AMENDMENT XIII

Section 1.

Neither slavery nor involuntary servitude, except as a punishment for crime whereof the party shall have been duly convicted, shall exist within the United States, or any place subject to their jurisdiction.

Section 2.

Congress shall have power to enforce this article by appropriate legislation.

Passed by Congress January 31, 1865. Ratified December 6, 1865.

AMENDMENT XIV

Section 1.

All persons born or naturalized in the United States, and subject to the jurisdiction thereof, are citizens of the United States and of the State wherein they reside. No State shall make or enforce any law which shall abridge the privileges or immunities of citizens of the United States; nor shall any State deprive any person of life, liberty, or property, without due process of law; nor deny to any person within its jurisdiction the equal protection of the laws.

Section 2.

Representatives shall be apportioned among the several States according to their respective numbers, counting the whole number of persons in each State, excluding Indians not taxed. But when the right to vote at any election for the choice of electors for President and Vice-President of the United States, Representatives in Congress, the Executive and Judicial officers of a State, or the members of the Legislature thereof, is denied to any of the male inhabitants of such State, being twenty-one years of age, and citizens of the United States, or in any way abridged, except for participation in rebellion, or other crime, the basis of representation therein shall be reduced in the proportion which the number of such male citizens shall bear to the whole number of male citizens twenty-one years of age in such State.

Section 3.

No person shall be a Senator or Representative in Congress, or elector of President and Vice-President, or hold any office, civil or military, under the United States, or under any State, who, having previously taken an oath, as a member of Congress, or as an officer of the United States, or as a member of any State legislature, or as an executive or judicial officer of any State, to support the Constitution of the United States, shall have engaged in insurrection or rebellion against the same, or given aid or comfort to the enemies thereof. But Congress may by a vote of two-thirds of each House, remove such disability.

Section 4.

The validity of the public debt of the United States, authorized by law, including debts incurred for payment of pensions and bounties for services in suppressing insurrection or rebellion, shall not be questioned. But neither the United States nor any State shall assume or pay any debt or obligation incurred in aid of insurrection or rebellion against the United States, or any claim for the loss or emancipation of any slave; but all such debts, obligations and claims shall be held illegal and void.

Section 5.

The Congress shall have the power to enforce, by appropriate legislation, the provisions of this article.

Passed by Congress June 13, 1866. Ratified July 9, 1868.

AMENDMENT XV

Section 1.

The right of citizens of the United States to vote shall not be denied or abridged by the United States or by any State on account of race, color, or previous condition of servitude.

Section 2.

The Congress shall have the power to enforce this article by appropriate legislation.

Passed by Congress February 26, 1869. Ratified February 3, 1870.

APPENDIX B

Document Transcriptions

Petition of Colored Citizens of South Carolina for Equal Rights Before the Law, and the Elective Franchise, 1865
(detail shown on page 89)

Justin S. Morrill Papers, Manuscript Division, Library of Congress, Washington, DC

To the Honorable Senate and House of Representatives in Congress assembled.

We the undersigned colored citizens of South Carolina, do respectfully ask your Honorable Body, in consideration of our unquestioned loyalty, exhibited by us alike as bond or free;—as soldier or laborer;—in the Union lines under the protection of the government; or within the rebel lines under the domination of the rebellion; that in the exercise of your high authority, over the re-establishment of civil government in South Carolina, our equal rights before the law may be respected;—that in the formation and adoption of the fundamental law of the state, we may have an equal voice with all loyal citizens; and that your Honorable Body will not sanction any state Constitution, which does not secure the exercise of the right of the elective franchise to all loyal citizens, otherwise qualified in common course of American law, without distinction of Color—Without this political privilige we will have no security for our personal rights and no means to secure the blessings of education to our children.

The state needs our vote, to make the state loyal to the Union, and to bring its laws and administration into harmony with the present dearly bought policy of the country, and we respectfully suggest that had the constitution of South Carolina been heretofore, as we now ask that it shall be hereafter, this state would never have led one third of the United States into treason against the nation.

For this object, your petitioners will as in duty bound, ever pray &c.

• • •

Diary of Frances Anne Rollin Whipper, entry from August 1–2, 1868 (detail shown on pages 94–95)

Collection of the Smithsonian National Museum of African American History and Culture, Gift of the Carole Ione Lewis Family Collection, 2018.101.1

1868
Saturday, August 1.

Raleigh

Arrived here about nine oclock this morn Went to Mr J H Harris' residence where I was most cordially received by him and his very amaible wife I soon felt myself at ease having refreshed myself I enjoyed my visit very much left at five oclock for Charlotte N. C. In the cars I was much anoyed by the stares of the poor whites. Such women abounded therein. reach Charlotte about 11 p.m.

1868
Sunday, August 2.

Columbia S. C.

Reached Columbia about six oclock Mr Whipper met me at the depot with his buggie, and took me to my boarding place where an elegant and spacious room awaited me. breakfast was tempting. My dear friend Mr Adams was in to see me very soon after my arrival. Charlotte came to see me in the morning but Kate did not. Went to Church in the morning with Harry Maxwell and Mr. Adams. The Gov and all the members were there. Quite an excitement created on account of the disappearance of Joe Howard after the visit of the Ku Klux Klan at night

• • •

Petition of a Committee of Freedmen on Edisto Island to President Andrew Johnson, October 28, 1865 (detail shown on page 138)

Letters Received by the Commissioner of the Bureau of Refugees, Freedmen, and Abandoned Lands, 1865–1872. Courtesy of the US National Archives and Records Administration, FamilySearch International, and the Smithsonian National Museum of African American History and Culture.

Edisto Island S.C. Oct 28th 1865.

To the President of these United States.

We the freedmen Of Edisto Island South Carolina have learned From you through Major General O O Howard commissioner of the Freedmans Bureau. with deep sorrow and Painful hearts of the possibility of goverment restoring These lands to the former owners. We are well aware Of the many perplexing and trying questions that burden Your mind. and do therefore pray to god (the preserver Of all. and who has through our Late and beloved President (Lincoln) proclamation and the war made Us A free people) that he may guide you in making Your decisions. and give you that wisdom that Cometh from above to settle these great and Important Questions for the best interests of the country and the Colored race: Here is where secession was born and Nurtured Here is were we have toiled nearly all Our lives as slaves and were treated like dumb Driven cattle, This is our home, we have made These lands what they are. we were the only true and Loyal people that were found in posession of these Lands. we have been always ready to strike for Liberty and humanity yea to fight if needs be To preserve this glorious union. Shall not we who Are freedman and have been always true to this Union have the same rights as are enjoyed by Others? Have we broken any Law of these United States? Have we forfieted our rights of property In Land?— If not then! are not our rights as A free people and good citizens of these United States To be considered before the rights of those who were Found in rebellion against this good and just Goverment (and now being conquered) come (as they Seem) with penitent hearts and beg forgiveness For past offences and also ask if thier lands Cannot be restored to them are these rebellious Spirits to be reinstated in thier possessions And we who have been abused and oppressed For many long years not to be allowed the Privilige of purchasing land But be subject To the will of these large Land owners? God fobid, Land monopoly is injurious to the advancement of the course of freedom, and if government Does not make some provision by which we as Freedmen can obtain A Homestead, we have Not bettered our condition.

We have been encouraged by government to take up these lands in small tracts, receiving Certificates of the same— we have thus far Taken Sixteen thousand (16000) acres of Land here on This Island. We are ready to pay for this land When Government calls for it. and now after What has been done will the good and just government take from us all this right and make us Subject to the will of those who have cheated and Oppressed us for many years God Forbid! We the freedmen of this Island and of the State of South Carolina— Do therefore petition to you as the President of these United States, that some provisions be made by which Every colored man can purchase land. and Hold it as his own.

We wish to have A home if It be but A few acres. without some provision is Made our future is sad to look upon. yes our Situation is dangerous. we therefore look to you In this trying hour as A true friend of the poor and Neglected race. for protection and Equal Rights. with the privilege of purchasing A Homestead— A Homestead right here in the Heart of South Carolina.

We pray that god will direct your heart in Making such provision for us as freedmen which Will tend to unite these states together stronger Than ever before— May God bless you in the Administration of your duties as the President Of these United States is the humble prayer Of us all.—

In behalf of the Freedmen

	Henry Bram.
Committee	Ishmael. Moultrie.
	yates. Sampson.

• • •

Hawkins Wilson letter to Chief of the Freedmen's Bureau at Richmond, enclosing Hawkins Wilson letter to Sister Jane, May 11, 1867 (detail shown on page 165)

Letters Received, Bowling Green (Caroline County, Assistant Subassistant Commissioner), Records of the Field Offices for the State of Virginia, Bureau of Refugees, Freedmen, and Abandoned Lands, 1865–1872. Courtesy of the US National Archives and Records Administration, FamilySearch International, and the Smithsonian National Museum of African American History and Culture.

[*Galveston, Tex.*] May 11th, 1867—

Chief of the Freedman's Bureau at Richmond;

Dear Sir, I am anxious to learn about my sisters, from whom I have been separated many years— I have never heard from them since I left Virginia twenty four years ago— I am in hopes that they are still living and I am anxious to hear how they are getting on— I have no other one to apply to but you and am persuaded that you will help one who stands in need of your services as I do— I shall be very grateful to you, if you oblige me in this matter— One of my sisters belonged to Peter Coleman in Caroline County and her name was

Jane— Her husband's name was Charles and he belonged to Buck Haskin and lived near John Wright's store in the same county— She has three children, Robert, Charles and Julia, when I left— Sister Martha belonged to Dr Jefferson, who lived two miles above Wright's store— Sister Matilda belonged to Mrs. Botts, in the same county— My dear uncle Jim had a wife at Jack Langley's and his wife was named Adie and his oldest son was named Buck and they all belonged to Jack Langley— These are all my own dearest relatives and I wish to correspond with them with a view to visit them as soon as I can hear from them— My name is Hawkins Wilson and I am their brother, who was sold at Sheriff's sale and used to belong to Jackson Talley and was bought by M. Wright, Boydtown C.H. You will please send the enclosed letter to my sister Jane, or some of her family, if she is dead— I am, very respectfully, your obedient servant,

Hawkins Wilson

[*Enclosure*]
[*Galveston, Tex.* May 11, 1867]

Dear Sister Jane, Your little brother Hawkins is trying to find out where you are and where his poor old mother is— Let me know and I will come to see you— I shall never forget the bag of buiscuits you made for me the last night I spent with you— Your advice to me to meet you in Heaven has never passed from my mind and I have endeavored to live as near to my God, that if He saw fit not to suffer us to meet on earth, we might indeed meet in Heaven— I was married in this city on the 10th March 1867 by Rev. Samuel Osborn to Mrs. Martha White, a very intelligent and lady-like woman— You may readily suppose that I was not fool enough to marry a Texas girl— My wife was from Georgia and was raised in that state and will make me very happy— I have learned to read, and write a little— I teach Sunday School and have a very interesting class— If you do not mind, when I come, I will astonish you in religious affairs— I am sexton of the Methodist Episcopal Church colored— I hope you and all my brothers and sisters in Virginia will stand up to this church; for I expect to live and die in the same— When I meet you, I shall be as much overjoyed as Joseph was when he and his father met after they had been separated so long— Please write me all the news about you all— I am writing tonight all about myself and I want you to do likewise about your and my relations in the state of Virginia— Please send me some of Julia's hair whom I left a baby in the cradle when I was torn away from you— I know that she is a young lady now, but I hope she will not deny her affectionate uncle this request, seeing she was an infant in the cradle when he saw her last— Tell Mr. Jackson Talley how-do-ye and give my love to all his family, Lucy, Ellen and Sarah— Also to my old playmate Henry Fitz who used to play with me and also to all the colored boys who, I know, have forgotten me, but I have not forgotten them— I am writing to you tonight, my dear sister, with my Bible in my hand praying Almighty God to bless you and preserve you and me to meet again— Thank God that now we are not sold and torn away from each other as we used to be— we can meet if we see fit and part if we like— Think of this and praise God and the Lamb forever— I will now present you a little prayer which you will say every night before you go to sleep— Our father who art in heaven &c, you will know what the rest is— Dear sister, I have had a rugged road to travel, since I parted with you, but thank God,

I am happy now, for King Jesus is my Captain and God is my friend. He goes before me as a pillar of fire by night and a cloud by day to lead me to the New Jerusalem where all is joy, and happiness and peace— Remember that we have got to meet before that great triune God— My reputation is good before white and Black. I am chief of all the turnouts of the colored people of Galveston— Last July 1866, I had the chief command of four thousand colored people of Galveston— So you may know that I am much better off, than I used to be when I was a little shaver in Caroline, running about in my shirt tail picking up chips— Now, if you were to see me in my fine suit of broadcloth, white kid gloves and long red sash, you would suppose it was Gen. Schofield marching in parade uniform into Richmond— The 1st day of May, 1867, I had 500 colored people, big and little, again under my command— We had a complete success and were complimented by Gen. Griffin and Mr. Wheelock the superintendent of the colored schools of Texas— We expect to have a picnic for the Sunday School soon— I am now a grown man weighing one hundred and sixty odd pounds— I am wide awake and full of fun, but I never forget my duty to my God— I get eighteen dollars a month, for my services as sexton and eighteen dollars a week outside— I am working in a furniture shop and will fix up all your old furniture for you, when I come to Virginia if you have any— I work hard all the week— On Sunday I am the first one in the church and the last to leave at night; being all day long engaged in serving the Lord; teaching Sunday School and helping to worship God— Kind sister; as paper is getting short and the night is growing old and I feel very weak in the eyes and I have a great deal to do before I turn in to bed tomorrow I shall have to rise early to attend Sunday School, I must come to a conclusion— Best love to yourself and inquiring friends— Write as quickly as you can and direct to Hawkins Wilson care of Methodist Episcopal church, colored, Galveston, Texas— Give me you P. Office and I will write again— I shall drop in upon you some day like a thief in the night.— I bid you a pleasant night's rest with a good appetite for your breakfast and no breakfast to eat— Your loving and affectionate brother—

Hawkins Wilson

Protesters, including Rev. Raphael Warnock, senior pastor of Atlanta's Ebenezer Baptist Church, march with Lezley McSpadden and Michael Brown Sr. in Ferguson, Missouri, August 2014, weeks after police killed their unarmed African American teenage son, Michael Brown.

BIBLIOGRAPHY

1865 *Petition from the State Convention of Colored People of South Carolina*. Scroll. Library of Congress. Washington, DC.

African American Policy Forum. "Say Her Name: Resisting Police Brutality Against Black Women." African American Policy Forum. New York. 2015. https://44bbdc6e-01a4-4a9a-88bc-731c6524888e .filesusr.com/ugd/62e126_8752f0575a22470ba7c7be7f723ed6ee.pdf

Ash, Stephen V. *A Massacre in Memphis: The Race Riot that Shook the Nation One Year After the Civil War*. New York: Hill and Wang, 2013.

Ayers, Edward L. *The Thin Light of Freedom: The Civil War and Emancipation in the Heart of America*. New York: W. W. Norton & Company, 2018.

Behre, Robert. "Historic Henry Hutchinson House on Edisto Island Now a Happy Camper as It Awaits Restoration." *Post and Courier*, October 14, 2020.

Bercaw, Nancy. *Gendered Freedoms: Race, Rights, and the Politics of Household in the Delta, 1861-1875*. Gainesville: University Press of Florida, 2003.

Berlin, Ira, Barbara J. Fields, Thavolia Glymph, Joseph Reidy, and Leslie S. Rowland, eds. *Freedom: A Documentary History of Emancipation, 1861–1867*. Ser. 1, vol. 1. *The Destruction of Slavery*. Cambridge: Cambridge University Press, 1985.

Blackett, R.J.M. *The Captive's Quest for Freedom: Fugitive Slaves, the 1850 Fugitive Slave Law and the Politics of Slavery*. Cambridge, UK: Cambridge University Press, 2018.

Blight, David W. *Race and Reunion: The Civil War in American Memory*. Cambridge, MA: Harvard University Press, 2001.

Brown, DeNeen. "How Recy Taylor's Brutal Rape Has Become a Symbol of #MeToo and #TimesUp." *Washington Post*, January 30, 2018. https://www.washingtonpost.com/news/retropolis /wp/2017/11/27/the-gang-rape-was-horrific-the-naacp-sent-rosa -parks-to-investigate-it/

Brown, Elsa Barkley. "Negotiating and Transforming the Public Sphere: African American Political Life in the Transition from Slavery to Freedom." *Public Culture 7*, no. 1 (Fall 1994): 107–146.

Christensen, Stephanie. "The Great Migration (1915-1960)." BlackPast.org. https://www.Blackpast.org/african-american-history /great-migration-1915-1960/

Corasaniti, Nick, Jason Horowitz, and Ashley Southall. "Nine Killed in Shooting at Black Church in Charleston." *New York Times*, June 17, 2015. https://www.nytimes.com/2015/06/18/us/church-attacked-in -charleston-south-carolina.html

Douglass, Frederick. "Our Composite Nationality." In *The Speeches of Frederick Douglass: A Critical Edition*, edited by George Barr, Eamonn Brandon, Kate Burzlaff, Mark Furnish, Julie Husband, Kathryn Jacks, Heather L. Kaufman, John R. McKivigan, Rebecca Pattillo, Alex Smith, and Lynette Taylor. New Haven, CT: Yale University Press, 2018.

Downs, Gregory P. *Declarations of Dependence: The Long Reconstruction of Popular Politics in the South, 1861–1908*. Chapel Hill: University of North Carolina Press, 2011.

Du Bois, W.E.B. "A Litany for Atlanta." In *The Book of American Negro Poetry*, edited by James Weldon Johnson. New York: Harcourt Brace and Company, 1922.

———. *Black Reconstruction in America: An Essay Toward a History of the Part Which Black Folk Played in the Attempt to Reconstruct Democracy in America, 1860–1880*. New York: Harcourt Brace and Company, 1935.

Dudden, Faye E. *Fighting Chance: The Struggle Over Woman Suffrage and Black Suffrage in Reconstruction America*. Oxford: Oxford University Press, 2011.

Edwards, Laura F. *A Legal History of the Civil War and Reconstruction: A Nation of Rights*. New York: Cambridge University Press, 2015.

Egerton, Douglas R. *The Wars of Reconstruction: A Brief, Violent History of America's Most Progressive Era*. New York: Bloomsbury Press, 2014.

Equal Justice Initiative. *Lynching in America: Confronting the Legacy of Racial Terror*. 3rd ed. Montgomery, AL: Equal Justice Initiative, 2017. https://eji.org/wp-content/uploads/2020/09 /lynching-in-america-3d-ed-091620.pdf

Equal Justice Initiative. *Remembering Black Veterans Targeted for Racial Terror Lynchings*. https://eji.org/news/remembering-Black-veterans-and-racial-terror-lynchings/

Estevez, George Gregory, III. *Edisto Island: The African-American Journey*. Self-published, 2019.

Feimster, Crystal. *Southern Horrors: Women and the Politics of Rape and Lynching*. Cambridge, MA: Harvard University Press, 2011.

———. "'What If I Am A Woman': Black Women's Campaigns for Sexual Justice and Citizenship," in *The World the Civil War Made*, edited by Gregory P. Downs and Kate Masur. Chapel Hill: University of North Carolina Press, 2015.

Foner, Eric. *The Fiery Trail: Abraham Lincoln and American Slavery*. New York: W. W. Norton, 2010.

———. *Forever Free: The Story of Emancipation and Reconstruction*. New York: Vintage, 2013.

———. *Give Me Liberty!: An American History*. Vol. 1, 6th ed. New York: W. W. Norton & Company, 2019.

———. *Reconstruction* Updated Edition: *America's Unfinished Revolution, 1863–1877*. New York: HarperCollins, 2014.

———. *The Second Founding: How the Civil War and Reconstruction Remade the Constitution*. New York: W. W. Norton & Co., 2019.

Franke, Katherine. *Repair: Redeeming the Promise of Abolition*. New York: Haymarket Press, 2019.

Franklin, John Hope. *The Emancipation Proclamation*. Wheeling, IL: Harlan Davidson, Inc., 1965.

Gardner, Eric. "Frances Ellen Watkins Harper's 'National Salvation': A Rediscovered Lecture on Reconstruction." *Commonplace: The Journal of Early American Life* 17, no. 4 (Summer 2017).

Gardullo, Paul. "Spectacles of Slavery: Pageantry, Film and Early Twentieth-Century Public Memory." *Slavery & Abolition* 34, no. 2 (2013): 222–235.

Giddings, Paula. *Ida: A Sword Among Lions*. New York: Amistad, 2009.

———. *When and Where I Enter: The Impact of Black Women on Race and Sex in America*. New York: William Morrow and Company, 1984.

Gidick, Kinsey. "Preservation as Witness." *Charleston Magazine*, March 2019. https://charlestonmag.com/features/preservation_as_witness

Glymph, Thavolia. "Noncombatant Military Laborers in the Civil War." *OAH Magazine of History* 26, no. 2 (April 2012): 25–29.

———. *Out of the House of Bondage: The Transformation of the Plantation Household*. Cambridge: Cambridge University Press, 2008.

———. *The Women's Fight: The Civil War's Battles for Home, Freedom, and Nation*. Chapel Hill: University of North Carolina Press, 2019.

Gorn, Elliott. *Let The People See: The Story of Emmett Till*. Oxford: Oxford University Press, 2018.

Hahn, Steven. *A Nation under Our Feet: Black Political Struggles in the Rural South from Slavery to the Great Migration*. Cambridge, MA: Belknap Press of Harvard University Press, 2003.

———. *The Political Worlds of Slavery and Freedom*. Cambridge, MA: Harvard University Press, 2009.

Haley, Sarah. *No Mercy Here: Gender, Punishment, and the Making of Jim Crow Modernity*. Chapel Hill: University of North Carolina Press, 2016.

Hartman, Saidiya. "Venus in Two Acts." *Small Axe* 26, vol. 12, no. 2 (2008): 1–14.

Hollandsworth, James G. *An Absolute Massacre: The New Orleans Riot of July 30, 1866*. Baton Rouge: Louisiana State University Press, 2004.

Holt, Thomas. *Black Over White: Negro Political Leadership in South Carolina*. Urbana: University of Illinois Press, 1977.

———. *Children of Fire: A History of African Americans*. New York: Hill and Wang, 2011.

Hunter, Tera W. *Bound in Wedlock: Slave and Free Black Marriage in the Nineteenth Century*. Cambridge, MA: Belknap Press of Harvard University Press, 2017.

Ione, Carole. *Pride of Family: Four Generations of American Women of Color*. New York: Harlem Moon, 2004.

Jeffries, Hasan. *Bloody Lowndes: Civil Rights and Black Power in Alabama's Black Belt*. New York: New York University Press, 2009.

Jones, Martha S. *Birthright Citizens: A History of Race and Rights in Antebellum America*. Cambridge: Cambridge University Press, 2018.

———. *Vanguard: How Black Women Broke Barriers, Won the Vote, and Insisted on Equality for All*. New York: Basic Books, 2020.

Joseph, Peniel. *Waiting Til the Midnight Hour: A Narrative History of Black Power in America*. New York: Macmillan, 2006.

Kantrowitz, Stephen David. *Ben Tillman and the Reconstruction of White Supremacy.* Chapel Hill: University of North Carolina Press, 2000.

———. *More Than Freedom: Fighting for Black Citizenship in a White Republic, 1829–1889.* New York: Penguin Press, 2012.

Keith, LeeAnna. *The Colfax Massacre: The Untold Story of Black Power, White Terror, and the Death of Reconstruction.* Oxford: Oxford University Press, 2007.

Keyssar, Alexander. *The Right to Vote: The Contested History of Democracy in the United States.* New York: Basic Books, 2000.

King, Martin L. "I Have a Dream." Speech presented at the March on Washington for Jobs and Freedom, August 28, 1968. https://avalon .law.yale.edu/20th_century/mlk01.asp

Leach, Nathan. "The Henry Hutchinson House." *Charleston Magazine.* March 26, 2019. Video, 3:02. https://www.youtube.com /watch?v=lWLAktLZm-4

LeFlouria, Talitha. *Chained in Silence: Black Women and Convict Labor in the New South.* Chapel Hill: University of North Carolina Press, 2016.

Litwack, Leon F. *Been in the Storm So Long: The Aftermath of Slavery.* New York: Alfred A. Knopf, 1979.

Lumpkins, Charles. *American Pogrom: The East St. Louis Race Riot and Black Politics.* Athens: Ohio University Press, 2008.

Marshall, Amani T. "'They Are Supposed To Be Lurking About The City:' Enslaved Women Runaways In Antebellum Charleston." *The South Carolina Historical Magazine* 115, no. 3 (July 2014): 188–212.

Masur, Kate. *Until Justice Be Done: America's First Civil Rights Movement, from the Revolution to Reconstruction.* New York: W. W. Norton & Company, 2021.

McLaurin, Melton A. *Celia, A Slave.* Athens: University of Georgia Press, 1991.

McWhirter, Cameron. *Red Summer: The Summer of 1919 and the Awakening of Black America.* New York: Henry Holt, 2011.

Mixon, Gregory. *Atlanta Riot: Race, Class, and Violence in a New South City.* Gainesville: University Press of Florida, 2004.

———. *Show Thyself a Man: Georgia State Troops, Colored, 1865-1905.* Gainesville: University Press of Florida, 2017.

Morgan, Edmund. "Slavery and Freedom: The American Paradox." *Journal of American History* 59, no. 1 (June 1972): 5–29.

National Parks Service. "Just as Well as He: Adella Hunt Logan." Tuskegee Institute National Historic Site. https://www.nps.gov /people/just-as-well-as-he-adella-hunt-logan.htm

National Coalition of Blacks for Reparation in America. "What is Reparations." https://www.ncobraonline.org/reparations/

Nunley, Tamika. *At the Threshold of Liberty: Women, Slavery, and Shifting Identities in Washington, D.C.* Chapel Hill: University of North Carolina Press, 2021.

Oakes, James. *Freedom National: The Destruction of Slavery in the United States, 1861–1865.* New York: W. W. Norton & Company, 2013.

Painter, Nell Irvin. *Exodusters: Black Migration to Kansas after Reconstruction.* New York: Alfred A. Knopf, 1977.

Patterson, Orlando. *Slavery and Social Death.* Cambridge, MA: Harvard University Press, 2018.

Puckette, Clara Childs. *Edisto, a Sea Island Principality.* Cleveland, OH: Seaforth Publications, 1978.

Rable, George C. *But There Was No Peace: The Role of Violence in the Politics of Reconstruction.* Athens: University of Georgia Press, 1984.

Ransom, Roger L. and Richard Sutch. *One Kind of Freedom: The Economic Consequences of Emancipation.* Cambridge: Cambridge University Press, 1977.

Reidy, Joseph. *Illusions of Emancipation: The Pursuit of Freedom and Equality in the Twilight of Slavery.* Chapel Hill: University of North Carolina Press, 2020.

Richardson, Heather Cox. *To Make Men Free: A History of the Republican Party.* New York: Basic Books, 2014.

Rose, Willie Lee. *Rehearsal for Reconstruction: The Port Royal Experiment.* New York: Oxford University Press, 1964.

Rosen, Hannah. *Terror in the Heart of Freedom: Citizenship, Sexual Violence, and the Meaning of Race in the Postemancipation South.* Chapel Hill: University of North Carolina Press, 2009.

Rosen, Kenneth R. "2 Charged in Confederate Flag Removal at South Carolina Capitol." *New York Times,* June 27, 2015. https://www .nytimes.com/2015/06/28/us/2-charged-in-confederate-flag-removal -at-south-carolina-capitol.html?searchResultPosition=4

Rudwick, Elliott, *Race Riot at East St. Louis, July 2, 1917.* Champaign: University of Illinois Press, 1982.

Saville, Julie. *The Work of Reconstruction: From Slave to Laborer in South Carolina, 1860–1870*. Cambridge: Cambridge University Press, 1994.

Senechal, Roberta. *The Sociogenesis of a Race Riot: Springfield, Illinois, in 1908*. Champaign: University of Illinois Press, 1990.

Shapiro, Thomas M. *The Hidden Cost of Being African American: How Wealth Perpetuates Inequality*. New York: Oxford University Press, 2004.

Sinha, Manisha. *The Slave's Cause*. New Haven, CT: Yale University Press, 2016.

Spencer, Charles. *Edisto Island, 1663 to 1860*. Charleston, SC: The History Press, 2008.

———. *Edisto Island, 1861 to 2006*. Charleston, SC: The History Press, 2008.

Stanton, Elizabeth Cady, Susan B. Anthony, Matilda Joslyn Gage, and Ida Husted Harper. *History of Woman Suffrage: 1883–1900*. Vol. IV. New York: Susan B. Anthony, 1902.

Steptoe, Tyina. "Ida Wells-Barnett (1862–1931)." BlackPast.org. https://www.Blackpast.org/african-american-history/barnett-ida-wells-1862–1931/

Sugarman, Joe. "The House That Hutchinson Built: Preserving a Touchstone to Edisto Island's Black History." SavingPlaces.org. https://savingplaces.org/stories/the-house-that-hutchinson-built-preserving-a-touchstone-to-edisto-islands-Black-history

Thomas, Gertrude. "Excerpts from the Journal of Gertrude Thomas." TeachingAmericanHistory.org. https://teachingamericanhistory.org/library/document/excerpts-from-the-journal-of-gertrude-thomas/

Twitty, Ann. *Before Dred Scott: Slavery and Legal Culture in the American Confluence, 1787–1857*. New York: Cambridge University Press, 2016.

United States. "Alabama: Testimony of John Childers." In *Report of the Joint select committee appointed to inquire into the condition of affairs in the late insurrectionary states, so far as regards the execution of laws, and the safety of the lives and property of the citizens of the United States and Testimony taken: made to the two Houses of Congress, February 19, 1872*. Washington, DC: Government Printing Office, 1872: 1719–1728.

———. "Georgia: Testimony of Warren Jones." In *Report of the Joint select committee appointed to inquire into the condition of affairs in the late insurrectionary states, so far as regards the execution of laws, and the safety of the lives and property of the citizens of the United States and Testimony taken: made to the two Houses of Congress, February 19, 1872*. Washington, DC: Government Printing Office, 1872: 689–692.

Ureña, Leslie. "Rosa Parks: Tired of Giving In." Smithsonian National Portrait Gallery. https://npg.si.edu/blog/tired-giving

Varon, Elizabeth R. *Disunion!: The Coming of the American Civil War*. Chapel Hill: University of North Carolina Press, 2008.

Wade, Lisa. "How 'benevolent sexism' drove Dylann Roof's racist massacre." *Washington Post*, June 21, 2015. https://www.washingtonpost.com/posteverything/wp/2015/06/21/how-benevolent-sexism-drove-dylann-roofs-racist-massacre/

Webber, Maggie L. "Grimball of Edisto Island." *South Carolina Historical and Genealogical Magazine* 23, no. 1 (January 1922): 1–7.

Williams, Chad, Kidada E. Williams, and Keisha N. Blain, eds. *Charleston Syllabus: Readings on Race, Racism, and Racial Violence*. Athens: University of Georgia Press, 2016.

Williams, Heather Andrea. *Help Me to Find My People: The African American Search for Family Lost in Slavery*. Chapel Hill: University of North Carolina Press, 2012.

———. *Self-Taught: African American Education in Slavery and Freedom*. Chapel Hill: University of North Carolina Press, 2009.

Williams, Kidada E. *They Left Great Marks on Me: African American Testimonies of Racial Violence from Emancipation to World War I*. New York: New York University Press, 2012.

Williams, Patricia. "Spirit-Murdering the Messenger: The Discourse of Fingerpointing as the Law's Response to Racism," *University of Miami Law Review* 42, no. 1 (1987): 127–157.

Wriggens, Jennifer. "Rape, Racism, and the Law." *Harvard Women's Law Journal* 6, no. 2 (1983): 103–141. https://digitalcommons.mainelaw.maine.edu/faculty-publications/51/

Zucchino, David. *Wilmington's Lie: The Murderous Coup of 1898 and the Rise of White Supremacy*. New York: Grove Atlantic, 2020.

CREDITS

Freedmen's Bureau office in
Richmond, Virginia, engraving
from *Frank Leslie's Illustrated
Newspaper*, 1866.

Convention Held at Cincinnati, Ohio, June 14, 15, and 16, 1876; 87:
Quotation from "Speech on the Eligibility of Colored Members
to Seats in the Georgia Legislature" by Henry McNeal Turner, 1868;
102: Quotation from "Self-Help The Negro's First Duty. Miss Ida B.
Wells Barnett Says Race That Will Not Take Initiative for Itself
Need Not Expect Aid from Others" in the *Washington Bee*, October
13, 1917; 119: Quotation from letter to Reverend M. E. Strieby,
December 17, 1866, sent by Edmonia Highgate. Letter from the
American Missionary Association Archives at the Amistad Research
Center at Tulane University; 143: Quotation from *Freedom: A
Documentary History of Emancipation, 1861–1867. Series 3, Volume 2:*
Land and Labor, 1866–1867 by René Hayden et al. © 2013 The
University of North Carolina Press; 159: Quotation from *All God's
Children Need Traveling Shoes* by Maya Angelou. © 1986 by Maya
Angelou; 174: Excerpt from "Elegy for the Native Guards" from
NATIVE GUARD: Poems by Natasha Trethewey. Copyright © 2006
by Natasha Trethewey. Reprinted by permission of Houghton Mifflin
Harcourt Publishing Company. All rights reserved; 187: Quotation
from *Black Reconstruction in America: An Essay Toward a History of the
Part Which Black Folk Played in the Attempt to Reconstruct Democracy
in America, 1860–1880* by W.E.B Du Bois.

CONTRIBUTORS

Kinshasha Holman Conwill is deputy director of the National Museum of African American History and Culture and is the former director of the Studio Museum in Harlem. She has organized more than forty exhibitions and often writes on art, museums, and cultural policy. A frequent lecturer and panelist, she is also the coeditor of *Ain't Nothing Like the Real Thing: The Apollo Theater and American Entertainment*, *Dream a World Anew: The African American Experience and the Shaping of America*, and *We Return Fighting: World War I and the Shaping of Modern Black Identity*.

Kimberlé Williams Crenshaw is the cofounder and executive director of the African American Policy Forum and a professor of law at the University of California, Los Angeles and Columbia Law schools. She is best known for her development of "intersectionality," "critical race theory," and the #SayHerName Campaign, and in 2021 received the Ruth Bader Ginsburg Lifetime Achievement Award from the Association of American Law Schools.

Spencer R. Crew is a museum director, curator, writer, and professor. Crew's career in museums began at the National Museum of American History where he curated the groundbreaking exhibition, *Field to Factory: African American Migration, 1915–1940*. He has served as director of the National Museum of American History and the National Underground Railroad Freedom Center and was acting director of the National Museum of African American History and Culture, where he is cocurator of the exhibition, *Make Good the Promises*.

Mary Elliott is curator of American slavery at the National Museum of African American History and Culture and cocurator of the *Slavery and Freedom* inaugural exhibition. She has more than twenty years of experience in presenting African American history and culture. Elliott's research focuses on antebellum slavery, Reconstruction, and African Americans in Indian Territory, with a concentration on community development.

Candra Flanagan is director of teaching and learning at the National Museum of African American History and Culture. Passionate about the sharing of history with K–12 educators, Flanagan has been instrumental in creating the Museum's portal "Talking About Race," a Web-based initiative that uses videos, role-playing exercises, and question-based activities to explore the origins and definitions of race and identity. She is educator for the exhibition, *Make Good the Promises*.

Eric Foner is DeWitt Clinton Professor Emeritus of History at Columbia University. A preeminent historian and authority on Reconstruction, he has published more than ten books on the subject, including one of the most influential, *Reconstruction: America's Unfinished Revolution, 1863–1877*. His book, *The Fiery Trial: Abraham Lincoln and American Slavery*, won the Pulitzer, Bancroft, and Lincoln prizes for 2011.

Katherine Franke is the James L. Dohr Professor of Law at Columbia University, where she also directs the Center for Gender and Sexuality Law and is the faculty director of the Law, Rights, and Religion Project. She is among the nation's leading scholars writing on law, race, religion, and rights, and is the author of *Repair: Redeeming the Promise of Abolition*.

Paul Gardullo, project director for the *Make Good the Promises* exhibition, is a curator of history at the National Museum of African American History and Culture and director of the Museum's Center for the Study of Global Slavery. His research and writing also focuses on the cultural memory of slavery in the twentieth century. He is the coauthor of *From No Return: The 221-Year Journey of the Slave Ship São José*.

Thavolia Glymph, professor of history and law at Duke University, studies the US South with a focus on nineteenth-century social history. She has published numerous articles, essays, and books, including *Out of the House of Bondage: The Transformation of the Plantation Household*, and also served as coeditor of two volumes of *Freedom: A Documentary History of Emancipation, 1861–1867*.

Hasan Kwame Jeffries teaches African American history at the Ohio State University, and is the author of *Bloody Lowndes: Civil Rights and Black Power in Alabama's Black Belt*. He frequently shares his research on the Black experience and insights on contemporary Black politics through public lectures, teacher workshops, and media appearances.

Kathleen M. Kendrick is exhibitions curator at the National Museum of African American History and Culture and cocurator of the exhibition *Make Good the Promises*. She is also the author of *The Official Guide to the National Museum of African American History and Culture*.

Kidada E. Williams writes about African Americans' experiences of racist violence after slavery. She teaches courses on African American history at Wayne State University in Detroit and is the author of *They Left Great Marks on Me: African American Testimonies of Racial Violence from Emancipation to World War I*. Williams was a codeveloper of the *Charleston Syllabus*, a crowd-sourced project that provides understanding of the historical context surrounding the 2015 racial massacre at Charleston's Emanuel African Methodist Episcopal Church.

INDEX

Page numbers followed by *f* refer to figures and captions.

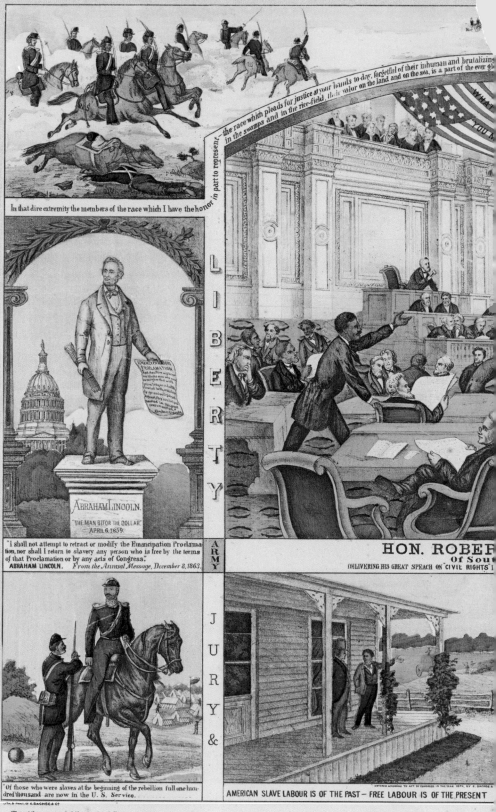

In that dire extremity the members of the race which I have the honor in part to represent, the race which pleads for justice at your hands to-day, forgetful of their inhuman and brutalizing in the swamps and in the rice-field, their valor on the land and on the sea, is a part of the ever glo

ABRAHAM LINCOLN.
"THE MAN BEFOR THE DOLLAR."
APRIL 6. 1859.

"I shall not attempt to retract or modify the Emancipation Proclamation, nor shall I return to slavery any person who is free by the terms of that Proclamation or by any acts of Congress." ABRAHAM LINCOLN. From the Annual Message, December 8, 1863.

HON. ROBER
Of Sout
DELIVERING HIS GREAT SPEACH ON "CIVIL RIGHTS" I

"Of those who were slaves at the beginning of the rebellion full one hundred thousand are now in the U. S. Service.

AMERICAN SLAVE LABOUR IS OF THE PAST — FREE LABOUR IS OF THE PRESENT

The rights contended for in this bill are among the sacred rights of mankind, which are not to be rummaged for among old parchments or musty records; they are written as with a sunbeam in the who-

THE SHACKLE BROKEN — BY

LITH. & PRINT. BY E. SACHSE & C?